DEAR **NWO,** I'M STILL HERE BITCH!

The detailed understanding of the plot to overturn the sheep.

ANN HAVEN

ARCHWAY PUBLISHING

Archway Publishing books may be ordered through booksellers or by contacting:

Archway Publishing
1663 Liberty Drive
Bloomington, IN 47403
www.archwaypublishing.com
844-669-3957

Because of the dynamic nature of the Internet, any web addresses or
links contained in this book may have changed since publication and
may no longer be valid. The views expressed in this work are solely those
of the author and do not necessarily reflect the views of the publisher,
and the publisher hereby disclaims any responsibility for them.

Any people depicted in stock imagery provided by Getty Images are
models, and such images are being used for illustrative purposes only.
Certain stock imagery © Getty Images.

Interior Image Credit: Ann Haven

ISBN: 978-1-4808-9551-5 (sc)
ISBN: 978-1-4808-9552-2 (e)

Library of Congress Control Number: 2020916998

Print information available on the last page.

Archway Publishing rev. date: 09/23/2020

for D ~

CONTENTS

PROLOGUE

Hello darkness, my old friend; yes Simon and Garfunkel said it best in describing the forever fog that follows me. Or was it Dexter that put it into words best? The dark passenger? Either way they all have a grasp of how it feels to walk in my shoes and yours if you're reading this. Should I make this an autobiography? Who am I? An autobiography is for famous people or those who have had a great success and people want to know how they've gotten there right? I am none of those. I could have been, if my father hadn't given me a major mental block on writing was a hobby and nothing to hold in high regard or to make a living off of. Nothing to stand behind with great pride and support; a useless waste of self. But in life, I'm a nobody writing about how I got to this point, a nobody, to you the reader. I am of great significance, but you don't know that, you just started reading. Let me slap the right and left hemispheres of your brain together through this and see if you come out feeling any different.

I am a believer that you have people in your life to complete something, maybe something of theirs. There are those individuals who come to strip you of doubt, fear, reasoning, thought, and even physical and verbal movement. You are then left with faith purely. There is only one choice because you've lost all the rest; with me, it was moving, speaking that helped me to reason. I have to learn to not rely on those people as, by any means not going to be permanent in this life. I am not meant for those relationships here. I just need to take those little moments and create a place of hope. To give people a touchable place I cannot grasp. I feel this will be no easy task. In becoming so bitter with the human race, I've noticed they look at me as the 'new plague,' quite literally. The disgust that overcomes their faces when I'm around. This is a great tool for me at times, and in the little pockets of time where I truly need someone it works against me. When you get some of life's secrets, and beg for just one person to share it with it seems you cannot. Why is that? Why is it when you embark on the most precious gifts of God himself that they are to be a secret? I want to experience them with another human at times, however the secrecy is flattering that I'm worthy of keeping it. Is that what I should do? Keep all the angelic secrets and experiences for myself? That is a lonely thought. Now you may think by me saying this I feel like I am superior to man in some way; quite the contrary. I pity them in a way, you see because some humans will never know anything past their own two eyes. I am however convinced these same asshole meat bags are smiling for the same reason and I intend to prove my theories. What theory you ask? Yes indeed, well one theory being that at some point they are all tempted by some sort of brain washing. It takes to some faster than others and then there are cases where it just takes more convincing that something will be promised to them. A sacrifice perhaps to save another human. It's only at the brink of terror and horror do they call for angelic help, and this is supposed to be their faith? Not good enough if you ask me. These humans are all placed into a category, categories which I believe fall back into the elements. Do you want to take the red pill?

INTRODUCTION

What is an Empath? A HSP? Borderline Personality, PTSD, energetic sensitivity and/or heightened awareness, lucid dreaming, astral projection, DMT, New World Order, symbology, karma, angels and Demons (not Dan Brown). That's me, trying to survive; that word: SURVIVE. I have on a loop in my head all day. How? With all that, how the fuck? How can I, the anger, and I understand anger is the goal for lower forces, but the red I see on a daily to just do basics are unreal. So no one and nothing stays the same. I understand this statement and accept it for a greater good. When it's a greater good. How often have we heard the sentence, "when I was a kid?" Right? Or "it never used to be like that!" as a whole, people still use this as a way of coping with change. And I don't know a parent or grandparent who has never said this to the next generation. The problem I have with "today" is its meaning. Again, I have a problem only if the greater good isn't a hypocrite.

Weak individuals standing together don't give the illusion of a strong mob. It's just easier to manipulate the whole. A mass of people that are weak alone can be easily persuaded. If we are down to verbiage, that's more than a scary place we live. That's beyond chess, that's extreme calculus bullshit; and I don't do math. And to trump that, I don't believe electronics. Mechanics yes, computers no. Weakened us after let's say 1995, we became its slave. I don't do slavery. To anything. No one should ever feel shackled for who they are. I am. Yes, I'm a white female, but I am a slave to many things. Traumas, disabilities, hush society, my body, my mind, and everyone I come in contact with. Because I HAVE to change all of it to function in the world? I have to deny who I am to work, to deal with the public, to have "any" sort of relationship whatsoever, to keep a therapist, to learn anything. Forget the luxuries I hear about: joy, love, family, marriage, friends, and career. Wishful thinking from "white privilege?" Say it. Because I know some of you reading this are thinking it. But all I've ever wanted in life: family, respect in career, and to make a difference. After pushing blood sweat and tears I've only gotten abandonment, silenced, homelessness, bankruptcy, poverty, discrimination and no "me too." I'll tell ya that much. Shall we touch on that for a moment? If you haven't burned this yet. At what point is anyone looking at a statute of limitations? I've been raped, no one gave a shit. Why? I waited less than a week to get it to the police. I've been molested by someone in power, a few times! No one gave a shit! Why are men losing their jobs over shit from 5, 10, and 15 years ago that happened in their personal lives?! So I'm torn here. You have someone assaulted and violated, report it. Go through your rape kit and the system, right then. You can't use that violation as an ace in your pocket for when you need it! Who's allowing that shit? NWO (New World Order)? Is there no investigation anymore? Where did this shift happen in the court system? Oh at your house okay, well he's fired. What?! What does that have to do with it? I can get on board more if he or she asked you to whip it out "for" the job or at the job site. Then I get how losing the job factors, but showing his junk at a party in '92, now he can't deliver mail seems farfetched. Please explain court system, or society, or whoever is making the rules for this crap now. Society will arrest me if I say the wrong word from the dictionary? Police will arrest me if I lose it on society for that freedom of speech. I'm fucked, or so they think.

Brings me to, how can you or anyone walk outside without a back-pack filled of anxiety about: "anything I do now (in this sensitive as shit society) could result in my arrest, or getting fired, or worse." How can I leave the house and deal with anyone without that fear? Now I'm not sure if this anger mixed with fear is present in every-one, but it's a constant for me. It's why I've been "diagnosed" with "mental illness" and a plethora of "disorders" to in my opinion make the outside world feel more comfortable with me. Certainly doesn't make me feel more comfortable. It shines a big spot light on me of "crazy bitch." When in all honesty, I think there are some serious issues with society, not me as an individual. Turn that light around; see that honest reflection from inside my mind. It may make "crazy" sense.

How do I work and make money? How can I be in public service? How am I supposed to help anyone in my current line of work if I'm being recorded for my verbiage, the way I touch you in healthcare? If I keep my head down and not talk to anyone, don't make eye contact, clock in and out; I've done it, I've been written up for being too angry. I'm walking on eggshells when I leave my room! Now let's add "my face" that reads: angry to people. Try probably constipated looking! Shit, try having all of that going on in your fucking head every minute going to work, driving to work, going to the grocery store. Living in fear anything you do or say is going to result in being arrested or fired. Yea, my facial expression probably doesn't read too great. I've gotten written up for that too. My "face" reads: angry, and I'm unpleasant to clients and patients. More like, I'm just being very fucking careful and purposely forgot to smile so no one thinks I'm flirting! We could add up how many times I've been in trouble at school or work or pushed out of a job, but the main point is, my personality and nature is on one side of the spectrum. This NWO doesn't have a box for me to be a citizen. Oh wait, I guess I could voluntarily check myself into a mental institute. But let's get real;

those people are on the out skirts of society. They aren't considered "members" or people really. Side note: no such thing is 'crazy' it's all spiritually related. So okay, accepting gay people now. Great. Finally reading Mr. Science magazines, good for you! Chromosomes, born that way just like heterochromia! I'm proud of you society. Guess we can't blame someone if their born that way. Look at society walking after crawling, I'm so proud!

HISTORY

Comedy, yes the world of my forever outlet from the world. I was raised on jokes, puns, pranks, you name it. Mostly of my own creation. SNL was my porn okay. I'd create skits with my father to get him to think I was worthy. Yes, it fed a LOT of emotional issues, but I worked the angle. I understood comedy, studied it like a serial killer does their victims. Now, something I refuse to accept (about NWO) is silencing. Silencing in general makes me go red, because I don't know how, but for the simple fact words now are being censored! Who's in charge of this bullshit? So, the sticks and stones saying no longer apply? What's the 2019 generation saying then? Sticks and stones are considered weapons, and words will result in you paying for my therapy?! I stand strong in believing 9/11 did a major domino effect to our country in reverse. Look at the timeline, did we really get stronger? Able to take more? Or did we become weaker individuals, and crumble at words? If this is hard to read, you won't make it through this book. A lot of pointing out hard to swallow hidden in plain sight realizations I've found will be revealed. Back to comedy, it's for people with heightened sense of intellect; and by saying this I am not implying this is me, there are plenty of comics I cannot understand nor keep up with. However it always has been from my seat this way and I hope that never changes. I feel when anyone gets offended by comedy they simply don't get that joke. In turn, have to then stand as if offended, to turn the tables, and make it into what it's not; a now serious comment or issue. What started as a comedy show is now a headline because an individual is simply not enlightened intellectually. If you're offended; you're not evolved as an individual, not as a society. This statement is harsh, but be real with yourself, is it true?

A lot of lost sleep when I was a kid, I remember that. I remember being scared at night a lot, so I'd stay up replaying steps of the day over and over again. Where I missed learning something, then having to fix it; Okay, I'll play that over and over again tonight in my head then wake up tomorrow and practice it. Playing everyone's conversations over and over again until they were memorized like a movie. From a clinical stand point this "programmed" me to be my own problem. I see it as a very well trained answer to a much bigger problem as I got older. I thank God a lot for the choices I was given for who raised me. You read that right, *the choices I was given for who raised me*, I will explain that meaning later. I didn't have the cuddly soccer mother; she wasn't in my life growing up. Emotionally unavailable, we were poor, drugs were involved, and it wasn't peachy. My dad re-married and started a new life once I reached pre-teen. I was on my own, or I saw it in many ways this way at age twelve. Here's a young girl, given a chart of life (I'll go into this in more detail later) at birth, fully aware what you're here to do. Get to the family, "hey, I got the answers, what does your chart say?" Fully trusting these people that are raising you right? Wrong! SO WRONG. In fact, these are the first people to teach you: deception, manipulation, abuse, sadism, narcissistic, addiction, demons, psychopath, sex and incest. A perfect environment for any little girl right? I will say this here, becoming a mother later in life having been through this and knowing where your spirit ports from and why it comes here (again I'll get into this more later) I fully, to my abilities, gave room for my children. I believe I did my job as a mother there. There was no way I was going to let another life enter with this bullshit if it were my responsibility. I'm in no way saying I didn't fuck up, because I have. But I've never crowded them as spirits, or treated them like less than what they were. Yes, they are my 'children' but that doesn't give me dictatorship over their spirits. Ever. I've always given room for that, because it's not about me when they are around. They are now here too, with their charts, their orders, and their insight. And it's *so* important to listen to, to compare notes, puzzle pieces are important individually.

In a perfect system of porting into 'Earth' every child would be placed with let's say a fully Enlightened family of acceptance, I got placed in the corrupt branch. Ok, I picked up on this a bit too late in terms of flat out acceptance after trying to change everyone's acceptance of not only just me but awaken them in some way to help them on their own paths. I got punished over and over again for this; I got the message, again too late. Fine it won't happen again, I walked, literally I ran away at thirteen. I must have got tired of knives held to my face from my grandmother, who knows; but I guess this was on her list! She was going to kill me; I remember thinking that; her own blood, if you stepped out of line. Just in an empire's point of view, I have to respect that woman for that; and to this day for a lot of reasons. She ran the tightest, systematic ship I've ever been a part of. I never agreed with one point on that woman's agenda, but I respected it, it was hers. I paid dearly for trying to change it and for being on it to begin with at times; but lived it, day in and day out. Studied it, worked for her, why? I was drafted into it. I turned ten or eleven and had some horrid fights with that woman trying to change that list so "I" could be a healthier person. The mental, emotional abuse that came from that is unreal. What is the take away? Don't change someone's path in life for selfish reasons. Never try to change someone for 'your' mental wellbeing. Simply, if I don't jive with someone for ANY reason, I can walk. I'm not about to do this battle again. The decades of therapy I have spent from trauma over her and my father alone, not to mention my mother issues (branching into women issues), abandonment, sexual abuse etc., but, and here is the huge ass in all rooms, it was only an issue when it was longer BLACK AND WHITE! When I tried to compromise with 'her' life list, ciao. If I questioned her rules of that house, she'd drive her red Cadillac up onto a curb a top speed yelling! Scared the shit out of me as a kid!

My assumption was she had the same birth chart I was given. As a kid, I didn't know everything I do now so I was naive in this thinking. Boom birth, let's do this chart list, fuck anyone who says no, or I'll grab a knife! I get it Grandmother, I do. What went astray, and again I thank God for this, is that her chart was far left (unpolitical) and white and I was sent in with far right and black. If she was smart, she would have accepted more puzzle pieces into the family and helped them find where their greater bunch is to fit. She was going to cut off any side of your piece that didn't fit to hers kind of woman! Can't ask questions in that environment, and no cliff-notes provided on what to do when you come in contact with an opposite.

In mating you blend it right? In cooking, mix it, see what happens. Try it. But trying to force two ends of a magnet? That's some science bullshit, and my high school science teacher was missing the front of his eyebrows. No one asked him, but everyone knew; you don't fuck with science. Everyone and everything has their spot, calm down. Just go door to door with your list like I did for a while, you'll find someone who can tell you where they're lining up for your color!

Despite getting placed in opposition at birth, it handed me great tactical advantages. I was a damn Russian Spy for another side for years. Minus the nightly water boarding, and getting locked in the bathroom when I got my first period like I was fucking Carrie, I was able to learn vantage points, figuratively and literally. See my step-grandfather, God love that man, recognized my grandmother's path; loved her dearly, had a damn near same list. They were in the same line. She had one son from a previous marriage, my dad from my blood line grandfather before he died when my dad was nine I believe, and then had adopted two more boys, a lot of charts, poor man. But he was the poster of what every step-parent should be. That dynamic is a long and hard road for a man unparticular. A man and woman, my views of the circle of trust (thanks DeNiro for this BTW), and all of you who are getting ready to read this and say, "It's not always a man and a woman, sometimes its two men." I do not hate on the gay community, relax, this is just a story and how I view the inner circle. It certainly maybe two same sex individuals, insert where you must here based on strengths. Man and woman have a child okay, the man is the sole protector, provider, fix all, pillage, hunt, insert stereotypes of say the fifteenth century. A woman to accompany her man of choice, to compliment her list*. Now you have a powerhouse, dynamic team. The goal of life becomes less of a burden when you as the man have direction where to point your sword (pun not intended), and women to be protected. Now if that concept makes you uncomfortable, go to therapy. But, to break it down, you shades of grey: this is if you have the same list, same job here, and same goals. If it's fundamentally different, I know from experience. Take mental notes, mimic, learn vantage points, and understand your enemy, and if they even are the enemy they can be a potential ally. Thy enemy of my enemy is always a potential ally, not my friend. The only friends you truly have are those willing to kill for everyone on your list, and I mean no questions, without hesitation. They know what you know; you were both there on sign up day. You study that policy and procedure book regularly. Quiz each other, talk extensively on every opponent and map out all of their potential vantage points and research clues of surrounding areas and groups; you are fucking Watson and Holmes in life. That is your friend, not, NOT based on a common enemy. That person will not question your judgement, or actions, for they are yours as well. That is your FRIEND. Feel yourself re-evaluate a few people after reading that? You might think, "No this is your mate, the one you marry etc." No, these are your friends, inner circle. A very tight place, all cut from the same fabric, but recycled as fuck. Now your mate, husband, wife etc., is that duo of the dynamic of male/female power (yes can be same sex) adjoining what I was talking about; then you have a child, let's add another layer. Bringing in the innocence, simplicity and all heart we forget as we age, very valuable in making decisions as a family unit; again, vantage points. But with anything: business, law, jobs, God. Children are a constant reminder God hasn't given up, and is ever present. Our gift is to give those children, all children freedom and security with that pristine chart a start. Carve out room, that soul is coming, and it doesn't belong to you! Pretty sure my grandmother thought all souls were hers. I'd joke she was a spawn of Satan in the flesh. But it wasn't far from the truth from this stand point. You had to believe what she did. Or that lady would water board you, hold knives to you, lock you in bathrooms until you prayed in silence: "God I don't mean this but I fear for my life…ok grandma…I agree with you." I am pretty good at hiding by the way, or she would then do a search and rescue on me. I'd hide from her when I couldn't take it anymore, and she'd find me every time. So her dynamic duo gets fucked, my grandfather dies of a brain aneurism, I'm guessing from holding it in so long agreeing with her over the years. Then you get a new man come in, enter step-parent, whatever dynamic is going on today with step-parents I don't know but this man knew what to do from my seat. My grandmother, still took a role as the woman; held one end of that pendulum every Monday morning at six a.m. and snap. It bounced to his end he knew where to point his energy and the three boys swayed in the middle. It sustained strategy throughout the entire week until settling on Sunday.

Sunday at my Grandparent's, Jesus! First of all, fuck panty hose for church as a kid. I was not a skinny kid, so panty hose and a short skirt wasn't a good choice at the store for starters. Know the body type you're dressing people. After ridicule of what a dumb-fuck I looked like was over to clothes they picked for me to wear mind you and we got to the church, I'm already making notes. I'm in Sunday school class to start off my life as a young child to give me a foundation of religion right? Not one person explains in detail what this thing is. Just, invisible duct tape over my mouth, you've been giving us resistance at home you must be evil go here. We won't be there, we'll be downstairs, and you go here. I actually had a priest come to my mother's apartment once to bless/mild exorcise me once. Well shit, my mouth was very chapped from the duct tape. That's not a possession, that's abuse and oppression; let's get that clear. Side note, the priest made me angry I remember that. For several reasons; for thinking I was possessed instead of abused, and for the simple obvious fact that man was unholy and I seemed to be the only one who knew it.

My hand kept going up and down during this Sunday school thing. Well shit, they had to take the invisible duct tape off when we went to church! Keep up appearances, fuck yea! I'm talking here. Now to be fair, 75% of everything I said was questioning the blatant form of all things that were in opposition which the stories were told. The rest, I was just glad not to have to be mute. But I was good at this, every damn word: "you just said the opposite a minute ago. Which is it?" "No I didn't." "I'm sorry, are you arguing with me, or yourself? Because you did." Bitch, I didn't write the lesson, you did! If you took the job teaching it seriously all I ask is that you're clear. Then I'd get: "well, it's all interpretation." "So now you're saying you did say two things in opposition, but it's up to me to do what?" "Just make your drawing based on the story I just read." "Lady, I'm trying, you still have given zero direction!" School ran like this too. EXTREMELY difficult for me to get a clear picture of what anyone wanted. No one was black and white, muddy as fuck and I was graded on that bullshit? Science, believe it or not was my best subject. Because it was subjective in a lot of ways for me, or I made it that way. When it came down to calculations on anything it seemed nothing was clear enough, even though numbers are supposed to be set in stone. When I needed to remember anything in school, I had issues recalling them for whatever reason. I didn't have an issue at home, but I couldn't apply this skill at school; it didn't carry over.

So when I was kicked out of Sunday school class to sit with my dad and grandparents downstairs, tension was high. The asking too many questions became "confrontational." You have to sing down there, and a lot of bad breath. Downstairs no one asked questions, just went along with every opposition the man at the front said. Oh I about came out of my skin. Is this the world? Do all these people agree? We go back to the house, huge breakfast every week. I fly to the room; get the damn crotch stifflers off my legs and into jeans. I'm going to find everything on what that man said, and prove it at breakfast. That'll earn me a spot at the round table with this family; I knew it. In some ways it earned me religious points, in others it was a fatal move. In retrospect, I should of started (and I did tempt making my mark with small things) with something of no value. But this, religion, God. Finally someone was speaking my language out loud! Let's go! I was a dog with a bone. And I never apologized for it, I never will. That's my chart, my list.

Because you see, for as far back as I can remember and even before going to Sunday school I could see-feel things. Children running in my grandparent's hallway, toys being played with in my closet in the room I had there when there weren't any, the black shadow behind my grandmothers recliner, eyes behind my mother's when she spoke, my father looking like a puppet at times when he was enraged. I never knew what any of it meant at the time, but when I started to read the Bible in Sunday school it intensified and started to make sense. The puzzle pieces of who I was going to become and who I was started to unravel.

I brought it up, bible in hand; the words the pastor said. Right there with every question. I was ready to show oppositions in his sermon, prepared for answers. My grandfather was helpful at finding scripture, always. Never quit helping me learn the books of the bible and verses, ever. God was with me that day and every day I challenged anyone. I took the punishment gladly, willingly even to be heard for that; and still. Not to say I'm right or wrong about any point, but to show where it's grey.

Whenever a sermon went grey, I was there questioning it. When anyone went grey with God, I'd fight, why? Because there is no grey, it's very clear. At birth, before that even; I've never been confused. One place I can say I am not, never not had a compass. But what was curious, is how mine was always pointing east first. Everyone muddied in this grey area did have a compass but theirs is pointed north first. Curious. So to me it got knocked off balance? Or was mine? Or am I fucking lost? What's going on here? No wonder why everyone was seeing a different color and waling left! No one was calibrated? Living in that house I was the brunt of abuse. Whatever my grandmother dealt with in her life was going to all come out on me and her kids. Which meant my dad got plenty of his own, and he found his dad dead on the floor at age nine I was told; so that carried over. My uncle even, when he was a kid got a fork thrown at him and it got stuck in his cheek by her. The torment over and over for years the both of them put me through is sick, twisted, and sadistic. But my mission was ingrained, I was put with these people either to help or learn. Try both if it kills me, at least I've done it in the name of God right? My grandmother hated my mother's family, for reasons I'm going to guess here from what I've gathered over the decades but also because it's probably for reasons prior to my birth I'm unaware of. Everything was a secret in both houses on family origin. Why? Good question. I had to dig, and dig past graves to find surface incest stories. So for years, and honest still to this day a part of me still believes two things: I'm adopted by one or both of said parents or I have a twin. Neither is true to my knowledge, but a gut, soul feeling says it to be true. Even though I've seen my birth certificate, I don't buy it. Something has never felt right about it. I think it's doctored. I just always felt I was ported into this shit show of a first family and didn't belong in anyway, and there was no evidence is to why.

She hated that family, hated was a light word for what I went through for being my mother's daughter that came from her pristine son. She was always conflicted with me, she loved one half of me to death, but any brief traits that showed of my mother would get punished; severely. My father had black hair, blue eyes just like her. My mother had reddish brown hair, green eyes. Here I am blue eyes dirty blonde hair! That was a trigger for her. So she would dye my hair routinely as a kid. And by kid I'm talking seven until ten or so when I could do it myself; and always cut it like a boys. I'll never forget what she'd say after it was done, "Now you look like your Daddy, not a whore like your mother." Just to be clear, that mind fuck on a kid, has layers.

She taught me to hate that woman right along with her. Deny all natural traits I may have that resembled her, mask the ones that did, and furthermore, how. I regret saying, it rolled over. My visitations with my mother were troublesome. All that anger went right along with me. I was my grandmother's little soldier; I was going into bat-tle the enemy! Looking back, a little girl fighting her own mother, and willing to do it for years, just to earn the worthiness at her grandmother's dinner table is disloyal. But it's how far manipulated

I had become, against my own mother. Just out of survival for self, not to be tormented anymore in that house I went along with it. To also attempt an alliance with at least one family member, my grandmother, my father; anyone I spent most my time with. To be considered as a valued member was important in that house.

There was one conversation I had with my father when I was young still, and he told me that feeling never ends, the need to please her. I can say, even years now, after she's gone, he's correct. That woke me up, to all of it at the time. If this isn't even a grooming process of a chair here, then what are we doing? Just abuse? For what? I had no parents, just training. No family, just training. I was alone.

My father did meet another woman. Oddly enough looked damn near exactly like my mother I'd like to think this was a smear to my grandmother, and a nod for my mom. I always smiled at this, and wondered if anyone else saw it. Oh lord, here we go on her story in my life. So at first, she was the mother I was missing for years. No games, warm, loving, no agenda, that I could see. She was pristine, not only just in appearance but appeared so in her life as well. Came from a warm family, full of hugs and smiles that had big family dinners and parties. She hid it well, or I didn't want to see yet another female figure let me down. Whatever the case, times were great at the beginning when her and my Dad were dating. I had moments that showed early on with her of mistrust and manipulation. I did test her, but only because it's what I knew. Also my grandmother was in on a lot during that time; also my mother had a few things to say. To be fair, a new woman to her ex-husband, that's understandable, but it was filtered through me to her. She got all of it, all of the neurosis of grandma and mom was put together in a series of tests for the girlfriend to prove her worth. Again, to be fair, the girlfriend didn't deserve that coming in as a new player, nor for me to track her progress. But this is how we (grandmother and I) worked.

How far can you be pushed? Do you crack? Where do you crack? Noted. Analyzed. Weakness. Remembered. We will use that later. Next subject, push it, how far? Oh I can go further with this, you're pretty comfortable there. Noted. Analyzed. Remembered. It painted a well thought out map of this person for us. Now we (grandmother and I) never spoke of this tactic, but this is how over the years I've put it together in silence. I studied how she worked, how everyone worked and made notes. Its tedious, but strong advantage in a lot of ways when you can do it quickly and have branched out on not just conversation; its everything. Movements, inflections in voice, eye contact, eye constriction, face flush, tone of voice, body positioning, shifting in your seat. That's only conversation body reactions, layer it with word choice and it's a whole new ball game. The meaning changes, you learn a great deal about a person with all of this on the table very quickly. Layer that even with intent, all of that match it with actions. Does it match with what they prove? I'm a mess I understand, but it's incredibly interesting how full of shit most people are. I'd like to say I'm pretty good at calling it, and my respect isn't given to many people.

I was in hopes the girlfriend was going to be the one to out rank my grandmother. She was passive aggressive, the first time I had seen this approach; warm, loving no agenda on her sleeve, no games. She was my hero, I'd never seen someone say fuck you lovingly; I loved her. She'd stop grandmother mid-sentence with something kind, but not really and smile! It was genius, I had to learn this. There was nothing we didn't do together; movies, Barbie's, tennis, shopping. Oh my God, I was a little girl! All this time I had been in boy clothes trying to look like my Dad and not my mother for my grandmother, or itchy panty hose for church. Girls don't wear swim trunks? What? Sweet! We are allowed popcorn at the movies? Grandmother usually weighed me before I ate, weighed my food, and then weighed me after. If I gained more than the food I had to skip the next meal and sit in my room to think about why I was fat whore like my mother. Not sure if I should be eating popcorn at the movies, let alone a soda! I stopped having friends come over to grandmother's to play because of that, she started weighing them too and compare us. Then remind me I'm the fattest one on the block. How am I explaining this to the girlfriend in line at concessions? If I take it and don't eat or drink it, then I'll have wasted her money, if I do, I'll be weighed in again, or what if this new lady does something worse? And she did, but I'll get to that.

Mom was always struggling financially; to be able to get enough cash to go to a movie was gold! We packed her purse full of suckers for that two time event. Unless her boyfriend was paying, then we were getting a soda to share for sure. Shit, what do I do here? The fucking guilt as a kid no matter who I was with was unreal, because every choice I made came with consequences.

The moment (and I'll never forget it, ever, because I'll always kick myself for not seeing it coming. All those years of training, and I even went against grandmother. Betrayed my first in command. For the good life, full of money, movies, no abuse, and guilt free popcorn. A kid fell for the oldest trick in the book, but the biggest lesson. And I'll have that look burned in my brain for eternity; the girlfriend gave me that look when that engagement ring slid on. It was past that joyful sparkle, past the bullshit excitement. It was her; it was raw intention. Damn it all to hell, grandmother called it. Now, after the picture I've painted of grandmother, you may have some dark opinions. Our family does for sure. But, I've always respected her. There are aspects of that woman that will always be unmatched. Respecting skills of thine ally will only make you stronger. Period. Not hate. Not envy. Remember that, learn the skills. What do they have you're so envious of? Learn it. Problem solved, for you. Enemy turned ally... you can use an ally; you cannot use an enemy if there is no common ground or skill.

I got played, or so she thought. The minute the ring slipped on, fun girl time ended for us. But if grandmother taught me anything it was not to be passive aggressive. And this bitch was, a skill to be learned yes, but I didn't have time. I was angry, and committed treason! Stepmom was going to get the wrath of not only my shit, but grandmother's and lets add some ex-wife envy from Mom fuel just for fun. I hope, to this day, as I saw who she was that day, she still thinks of the look I gave back at her. It makes me warm and fuzzy inside thinking of it. Call me evil if you wish, I'm comfortable with judgement. To cross grandmother, was pure hell, I lived it I know. It was day in, day out, waterboarding one fuck up; every angle, on how it was wrong. How she was right and she always had an argument on when you thought you were right. No, she had you there too, she already thought of it. I only had her on the Bible, I loved it too much. Stepmom wasn't making it out alive, no way. First call was to the chief after the night of the engagement. Of course she knew, that woman knew everything. I was still in purgatory for turning on her for stepmom in the first place, but I did have a plan. Tell chief I was only pretending to be on her side for information to bring to her; a spy. I mean, has anyone offered this to her before so blatantly? It could work. I mean she was bribing me to do it with Mom my whole life, why couldn't I do the same? She bought it! Now, here's where it got interesting; I told stepmom basically the same thing. Told her if she wants to be head chief so to speak, we need to put a lid on grandmother's antics. There I was a double agent age eleven for a year. Planting seeds for my true plan of my own. BREAK OUT.

The seeds were to drive grandmother away, and somehow get me out of the fake family set up stepmom used me for. Why was it fake? The minute that ring went on her finger: no more quality time just the two of us, no more shopping, no more Barbie's, no more movies. Bonding quality time abruptly stopped cold turkey, and I lost my friend. I told that woman stories, confided in her, trusted her. I was used to show she'd be a good mom to be a wife. Period. Had nothing to do with me; I wasn't even invited to the wedding.

Stepmom planned on having a baby and I'm sorry, but no; that was adding insult to injury at this point. Not only was I not good enough as the kid, but now we are starting over? I've worked a decade for a spot here! You don't just come in, toss some popcorn, and get me to betray all I've gone through just to erase me! I make that decision, and the driveway will burn on my way out. But okay, if that's what you're saying, I hear you loud and clear.

Stepmom was very step ford wife; very proper etc., I knew that well at grandmothers. Where each fork went at the dinner table etc., it was always extremely formal. Stepmom was Catholic; grandmother was Baptist, very different. But it seemed all religions to me no one was ever truly reading that book! That black and white book. Here's where I could scare the shit out of Dad and stepmom, drive out grandmother and win; again, God was there.

So, I read Revelations; then I read it again. Then I incorporated it into my daily life at home, and anything else I could find. I studied demonology, which actually was just helpful (learn thine enemy). But to Dad and stepmom I was "a bad kid" "in with the wrong crowd" and I was, but I needed to research it to learn it too. I belonged to God, and that was all I needed to know, I was on mission in that house and simply doing enemy research. To be fair, on the outside, it did look physically that way; but most judgements do at first. I studied everything dark during this time, and it is true: if you go looking for it not only do you find it, but it then sees you.

I fed grandmother so much information, just like she water boarded me, and I did it to her. When I couldn't to go to her house, I'd call: "Stepmom did this; I think she's trying that." Over and over, every detail. Then finally, news broke: grandmother and grandpa were moving to Arizona! Why? Stress. I had done it! The moment they left I turned to stepmom and said, "Your welcome." But it wasn't for her; I let her think it, while the second half of the plan was developing. She almost lost my brother from all I put her through I think, I don't feel an ounce of pride in that. It was a rough pregnancy for her. My brother was just born when Dad started referring to me as "the bad seed."

One day I packed a backpack, kissed my baby brother on his head and walked out. It wasn't until three a.m. until I surfaced. I got caught in my boyfriend's basement by his mother and kicked out on the street. I got one phone call, to my sister before anyone knew where I was.

My sister was my Mom's other daughter from a previous marriage. She's eight years older and growing up, I idolized her. It was the eighties, and having her big hair and style was what I strived for; everyone did then. Visiting my mom, she had the girl clothes and makeup; she got to listen to rock bands. At my dad's there was only The Beatles and Righteous Brothers and reading his books which were limited to the dictionary, thesaurus and Greatest Poets; it was dry to say the least. I bugged the shit out of her as any younger sibling does. Before stepmom she was the only female I trusted. Never displayed any betrayal. Nothing I said to her was used against me later for her own benefit. It was honest, real. The only person I'd let touch me physically. I'd beg to sleep in her bed at night, snuggle up to her, smell her. The smell of her skin to this day still brings a tear to my eyes, even writing this; because I know her smell. My safety, my sister. I know her hands, nothing about her was threatening.

With her, I could sleep, the only place I could. Attack or possible attack was always everywhere else. It was always her I called when I needed retreat; and I did it many times throughout my life, up to a point. That will be a theme throughout this, and you will see it's mainly women.

I now have, forgive me feminists, have formed and adversity to women. A very strong opinion of my own sex, and to very good reason; we break code. We are the quickest to break team, to change our "minds" and feel for another member. I've done it, it's in our nature, and it's the DNA. We are too fluid and willing to nurture to stand up to anything. I'm against women as Alpha for this reason. We give great direction and manipulation where men are blind, yet because of wanting to be all-inclusive let enemies in. Dangerous grounds. Men give a united front keeping zero emotion a factor. Safer grounds. I bet on that, not something that can potentially change and put me in harm's way. Possibly reasons I don't fully trust any air or water sign, they are too fluid in decisions. You can always bet on an earth sign, just a side note.

Why didn't I call Mom that night? She was always very involved with a boyfriend, or herself, or smoking pot, I couldn't trust it. The focus was fuzzy, and never on me, more for show. I never was a focal point for anything real. I was more used as a power move, not once did anyone care about my growth or emotional wellbeing. What was going on in my head was only questioned when I acted out. Why? Because it now was a reflection on others, not what could be going on with their little girl? Mom was bouncing from living with boyfriends, so when I'd go to visit I'd sleep on the couch in the apartment on display. The boyfriend and his son would wait for my shower to be over to see if I remembered clothes and "conveniently" be in the dining room when I got out; but not for the next two hours where they'd be in their bedrooms with the doors closed. Or "accidently" see if the bathroom door was locked while my shower was running, sure thing. Watching TV while I was trying to sleep on the couch, good times.

I really did hate most men she dated, but every once in a while I tried to do the right thing and have "family time." She dated one for years, and we'd get into wrestling matches. This one day he pinned me down, had an erection and put his fingers on my lips before letting me up. Later I told Mom, I said how they smelled like butt. I wish I could remember how blasé she was in her response, "oh it was probably from me, how funny." Or the time she found pictures in one of his pockets of him naked with two other women and showed me and my sister. To get our opinion of position? The photoshoot? What's the motive here? Right.

We took a trip back east to visit this boyfriend's family one year, the both of them smoking God knows what in the front seat. We get there, this guy has a brother that stared a lot; great. Everyone starts pushing me to go four wheeling in his jeep. This man is in his thirties, I'm pre-teen. We were alone! Mom doesn't know him, and no one is giving a shit. Not even this guy's wife! He pulls off in a cemetery, I get fingered, and he leans over and sucks his fingers right in my face. Didn't know what the fuck to do; I'm a child. Do I tell Mom? Based on how she reacted to her own boyfriend's wrestling match, this is probably a normal thing; so that's out. I'll just get home and tell my sister; and I did. Where that went, I couldn't tell you, but I did tell her. But nothing came of it that I know of.

My sister had moved out of our Mom's already a couple years by this point, and I can see why. I remember this time being very angry for me she moved into her own boyfriends whom she met earlier in a unique way.

Enter my Brother (in-law).

Prior to this current boyfriend my Mom was with another man whom was a small time bodybuilder locally here in Seattle. There's a small story of yet another boyfriend and my Dad that I'll touch on later. This boyfriend and a man were competitors in body building from what I know, or just did it together (I was very young so this is my recollection), but friendly at the same time. The man had come to a dinner at the apartment one night it was the boyfriend, Mom, my sister and little nine year old me. I'll forever remember the impression this other man had on my sister and me. She grabbed me, pulled me to the stair well and said, "Look at him isn't he gorgeous?" I said, "That man Mom's boyfriend brought to dinner? Ewe no!" I should have known then, that look in her eyes said nieces for me.

Over the next couple years Mom left that boyfriend and we moved out, but my sister started dating that man. I was on defense because who is this guy? Can we trust him? My sister was all I had! How can we randomly trust someone into the sisterhood here? Is this sister love one-sided? Thief! What the fuck was I going to do? The panic was on high and the anger pointed in one direction. That man.

He handled it very well, in hindsight. Looking back and we talked in length of this time and my guilt of it. He was very aware of the dynamic of not only everyone's position, but who I was. Acknowledged it through all of my fighting him early on; because I needed it. He sat and let me entertain him at dinners. When we went to the mountains all together, I performed little dance skits; he cheered me on. Stick on a cassette tape and show off some dance moves I learned, tell him jokes. I was warming up, slowly, very slowly; but I was warming up. Zero advances sexually, he was being very inclusive with my sister and my relationship; unlike my stepmom. Curious, what's this guy's game? I fought it for a long time, fought him for a long time. A LOT of their relationship, then when they got married I fought simply for the PTSD from what I had just gone through with my Dad and stepmom was present with my sister and this man. None of it was fair to them, but present. I was fucking scared I was reliving the same scenarios over with the both of them. So at every turn, I fought; it was all I knew how to do.

What was the best part? He let me; I'll never get to tell him what that did for me growing up, or in my life. He validated me at every turn. He saw who this little girl was; he never lost focus or shifted it. Saw I had a little talent and made everyone watch. In a family of "all about me" and "take all" for power play, you can see how infuriating of a crowd someone coming in shifting that away would make. He was over 250lbs., solid muscle, African American in a group of Caucasians. No one wasn't going to listen to him, well, anywhere. That man had presence with a smile; the kind the Rock Johnson has, where you wouldn't want to see the bad side so you just agree.

He used to be a cop before he met my sister, so demanding presence, plus his sheer size was just effortless. He saw my attempts to be heard, and never failed to wait and hear me as a human, he gave me that. Up until him this practice was foreign to me, I'd never been acknowledged as human before, just commodity. If I was trained right, anything I said or did will be used against me in the court of family, and there will be punishment for showing weakness later. So I'd want to, but fight him for trying to love me. Grandmother hadn't moved to Arizona yet when I first met him, so I paid for not only talking to someone of color, but for my sister's too. I paid dearly for loving either of them, any of them; and for sticking up for them and for what was right. Fighting, all I knew.

When I ran away, the call was to my sister and my new brother; my safe haven. My sister was then pregnant for the first time and her and my brother picked me up on the street down town and I went back to their house. I remember my sister being quiet the whole car ride and my brother yelling. I remember thinking, "this is the day I die. He will kill me for bothering either of them with my bullshit. Like I'm some major deal here, disrupting anyone's life for this run away shit. They are pregnant and here is this kid fucking with our lives." But it was that night, which my heart shifted with him, and my eyes were wide open. He said the following: "how could you do this? You pull your sister in the middle of the night in a shitty part of town where something could happen to her, my baby! Why would you put yourself in this area of town? In this kind of danger? Sitting on the side of the road?! No one here to protect you? Anything could happen to you down here!" That, was the most unselfish thing anyone had ever spoken to me in my life, and it was spoken during a fit of anger. Which to me said this man is me at the core, and who is better to be with for my sister than someone just like me to keep her safe? I remember all of my nervousness lifting at that moment in the backseat, and going completely limp. Even during his fit of anger, I just sat there staring back at him with shock and gratitude. And I could have hugged him at that moment; tears ran not of being scared out of his rage but out of his purity of heart.

He didn't mind so much I was being stupid, but that I wasn't being safe. Up until that point, I'm not sure if I even cared about that fact; physically anyway. I was very busy on mental and emotional attacks. I was very good on body language up to this point but never had a care about my physical wellbeing, and then there was him. A whole new aspect to me, but not the last.

My mother and I, over the next year or so ended up getting the rest of my clothes from Dad's (I had to turn in my key over to him after the running away like I had moved out of a landlords building) and go live with her and her boyfriend where I slept on the couch.

It wasn't long before that relationship turned bad and we lived with my brother and sister for a short time. This is the time my brother and I got to spend real quality time. This is where I learned how to take care of myself physically. He taught me about food, exercising, prayer regularly, and the hugest part of my life: family. Here is where shit got sticky, or it's where I can pinpoint, but you decide.

He was my brother (brother in-law), my sister's husband at this point, father to my niece, and forever a unique partner to me in this world in a lot of ways. But not how you'd twisted thinkers would assume, I'll explain to you open thinkers and try to put it in simpler terms for you. The time we lived with them were the most amazing, we bonded on a deep level. I'm talking every night almost, neither one of us would stop communicating about God and family. We saw it the same, no shitting you. All of those times I'd been trying to convince grandmother, this man had been doing it too in his own way. But the exact same notes for the both of us. On the Bible, human behavior, all of it; I mean dead on, it was one thought. We'd cry, laugh, and simply be in amazement over it. Well I would, I saw that man tear up twice. But he was always moved by the spirit of us, I do know that, I was there. We pull out books, look up ideas; this man had a book on everything! I was so impressed by that. Map it out, draw it out; then reflect on our own situations, and how members of the family currently fit; who we were in it. To be frank, this was felt, noticed, and discussed that it was unappreciated by observers around us. Still to this day the fact that we talked still pisses everyone off, and we had to defend it. Honestly, that's fine, I'm so fucking proud of whom we were to each other, and to research in general, I'll continue to do that. Yet I shouldn't have to, everyone around us should just respect everyone; we did. Period. We invested rather than arrested our friendship. And fuck me hard if those two didn't end up getting a divorce! After ten years I believe, not only did that single act cause my own PTSD issues, but now the only real family unit I had must be based on a choice? Now I'm forced to pick between my sister and my brother?! I was literally asked by my sister to pick a side, him or her, and to that I basically said: FUCK YOU! And that's how I felt, no matter the circumstances, no matter who did what to whom. I'm not losing again, number one, and number two I'm not losing my best friend. The only person that's worked as hard as I do on anything!

My brother and I have the same chart, same list. We mapped it out! Shit was damn near identical, minus a few astral differences. Plus, we learn new skills from each other, are you out of your fucking mind asking me to drop that just because a paper in the human world is signed? You're out of your mind. That's my partner in spirit crime! Bonus, we think every dumb-ass thing you people do is funny as shit, so we're always entertained. I'm not giving that up for anyone. Have any of you invested in ME like this spirit has? No. So how can you expect it? Furthermore, how can you turn your back on him after all he's done for you? Fed you when you were hungry, given you a place to live, enriched your soul, and kept you safe at night. I'm not forgetting any of those things, and I'm not turning my back on them. I'm loyal to the work, not the words. And his work to show love drove me to tears so many times; I literally couldn't bare ever not standing against him. What has everyone else proven to me? That you'll turn on me at any given chance to gain something for yourself? To make you look good? He, not one time, did that to me; even when I made horrid mistakes. Did we both fuck up against each other? Sure. I did majorly. But I will say this; it was never one against one. Someone was always influencing in on our loyalty with each other. He and I would have NEVER ever had a conflict, nor faltered in loyalty, if, there wasn't another player trying to gain an "I'm better" loyalty card. That was always what led to one of our major fuck ups that led to an explosion. One or both of us would somehow get manipulated, and explosion of disloyalty. If we both stood fast in solid, there never would have been any issues; zero. And I accept full responsibility for my disloyalty on my parts. I was smart enough to see the manipulation, yet put in positions where lives were being threatened. At some point, the heavy hand needs to come from the one who isn't the body builder to say enough; too far. I was never one to try to control him, but two times he went too far. Just two, in the entire time I knew him and I pushed back hard and firm and was met with his bad side. I made my fucking point, but fuck if he never shut up about it. Just admit I'm right, you went too far, you tell me all the time when I do it and I accept it. I learn from it. Grow damn it, it doesn't mean I don't love you. It did however to him, and I understood that for a long time. A LOT of back-pedaling for a long time. But I was willing to do it, because who we were and how we fed each other I knew was more important that any worldly grudge. He would see it too, and he did. But we both went through betrayals during that divorce. No matter how much explaining, that left a mark on us both. Who we were to each other wasn't going anywhere; no one it seemed was making that go away. When he died, I was asked not to attend his funeral. When he went into the hospital I was not called. I only knew from a posting on Facebook. No one called, not one person. I'm holding onto that anger for reasons I'm not sure of, but I know there's a place to let that out one day. It barely showed itself when I showed up to his side that day. My sister, Mom, my nieces, his brothers, his sons, and his new fiancé were all there. I have no idea what I looked like, but fury probably isn't too pretty. That day in the hospital was one of the only times I'd ever touched him, lying in that hospital bed. Yes you hug hi and bye, or at Christmas or whatever, but it was an "ass-out" awkward hug with us. And "ok, let's do this, it's Christmas" hug. Nothing either of us did, we weren't physically affectionate people. But that day, that wasn't my brother. My eyes staring at his hands I'd looked at for years, his finger nails, and his hair on his arms. Every arm muscle, his collarbone peeking out the hospital gown I'd sometimes see when he'd wear his gym shirts. His lips when he'd talk to me for hours and I'd hand on every word, the way his nose hairs were and he'd always grab at them. His eyelashes and how they look exactly like my nieces. His eyes closed now, little innocent brown wonderment I always thought. The same look my nieces have. Up to the tattoo on his forehead. I closed my eyes and felt us go. Held his hand, kissed his cheek, leaned in and whispered, "Seriously man, don't do this to me." Looking back now, how selfish. He was gone the next morning.

It's been 1,128 days since writing this.

I have not changed since walking out of that hospital. He was my partner in the spirit world.

I have become something else.

I was a mess that first week, and then I was running on anger for a solid year. No outlet; remember I wasn't allowed to be involved in any "family" services. So just an "outsider" running on pissed off rage. I took three days off from work to scream, then went back as if nothing happened. I got really thin, lost fifty pounds and months later diagnosed with stage four cervical cancer. Now I get to prepare for my own death, which honestly wasn't sure how to carry on without my brother so I was happy about in a lot of ways.

I go in after four days of screaming in the tub trying to have a bowel movement at home to the E.R. on a Monday morning. Urinating and defecating was impossible at this point, I was sure I had some sort of obstruction.

After the emergency room ran a CT, blood work and ultrasound, they forwarded me onto oncology. My boss at the time was pissed;

missing three days was sac religious at my job at the surgery center. I get there, and I'm up in stir-ups to have a gynecological exam. "Yes, I see it, it's bad. I'm going to stage you four." Then does a biopsy, of which I thought I peed after all over her table. Her assistant helping wipe me up. "I'm so sorry." I said, as I'm crying in pain. It was horrific when I sat up. It wasn't pee; it looked like I'd just given birth on the table, blood everywhere.

"You have stage four cervical cancer, if we aren't fast in treatment you don't have much time." "Wait, what? No, I just can't poop! What are you talking about?" "Mam, we need to go talk about chemo, please get dressed." I asked her assistant if she'd ever been wrong, if this could be a mistake. I mean, we hadn't sent any labs off yet! She reassured me she had been in practice for a long time and was never wrong, and by the looks of it, it was aggressive. "What does cancer look like? Can you take a picture for me?"

Over the next six months I went through losing my job due to not being able to work per doctors' orders, which led to losing my apartment. I was homeless, jobless and trying to die. I'd come to an agreement with my ex-husband to move back in with him and the kids to "live out my days." She also had put me on Dilaudid, a never ending prescription of medical heroine for the time being. Now I've masked plenty pain over the years with alcohol, and it did give me peace for a moment. I understand the use of drugs or alcohol; it clouds who you are or what is going on. But it also clouds what you're meant for and above all, wastes fucking time; allowing spirits and demons to enter your being. Sacrificing your ability to keep the wall up against enemies is man's downfall. For what? A fun time?! A party?! To have some 'me' time? It's weak, we are soldiers. Period. There is no me time. There is no joy, or anything you can keep for yourself. You work for God. The funniest part, I think, of that statement, is even to people that think they are working for themselves or their religion, or the devil himself; your still working for God. Think about that. If, one power, one creator, made it all happen from the start yes? Just that one thought, written word, not anything else. Can you honestly say, think, feel, ANYTHING that was made from there isn't working for it? Good, bad, evil, hell, heaven, all of it? It's all for one. As twisted up as things get and go, and get lost seemingly, and hide and lie to themselves. Sorry; in the end, one boss. That shit is black and white. So whatever you want to tell yourself, or hide with drugs and alcohol; just saying.

After six biopsies, planning my death, telling my kids, a drug addiction, no job, no place of my own to live, final results came in: no live cancer cells to move forward with chemotherapy. I get a call from oncology: "if you don't have cancer, she can't treat you anymore. Maybe try Endocrinology. Thank you." End of prescription, zero help on coming "off" an addiction, just "bye." Not that my entire life and family was fucked, just "bye." It was bullshit, that somehow that was lawful. She ends up calling me three months later to offer to give me a hysterectomy, something I asked for at the beginning and she refused. So I went ahead with it because the tumor was still there. I cyst was still present on one ovary, which later gave me another ER visit for a tubal torsion the following year. That plus during my P.E.T. scan numerous flags were risen that were ignored and swept under the carpet with her and my numerous primary doctors since. Presence of this "disease uncategorized" by a pathology lab in California, that was present all throughout my cervix, esophagus, aortic valve, throat, right leg, and dozens of lymph nodes. But not one doctor wants to touch it. Not one. Nor does anyone want to say what's going on, still to this day.

When I had a "cancer free" if you want to call it that, I don't because it's uncategorized, my living situation came to a grinding halt. My job was given away, so I had to look for work and move. I did so quickly and within six months I was in a car accident. My car was rear ended and totaled and my job gave me an ultimatum: quit or get fired. You cannot perform the job duties hired for on this doctors note for light duty. It's unacceptable. Again, how is this lawful? I had to move back in with my ex-husband.

Now I can't find work for many reasons, the theme of this book ("mental illness" I have severe issues with going outside), I've been in and out of physical therapy, there is no such thing apparently for disability for people like me because I keep getting denied, and I can't find work I'm assuming because my resume reads as a liability.

There was a first first boyfriend after divorcing my dad for my Mom, he had worked or owned a pizza restaurant up the road with a buddy; they had the best meat ball subs ever made. Also they had a juke box and pin ball, so I didn't mind at all going there. I must have spent a months' worth of laundry quarters playing Bon Jovi's Livin on a Prayer on that juke box. We'd go visit him and at times my mom would leave me to help out in the back. Now this was everything; I was determined to make him my husband one day. I laugh at this little girl crush now, but back then it was very serious business. I'd cry about it, I was a mess over him. That break up later was hard on me to get over. But I didn't hear from him much, aw my first broken heart.

Now later in life, he made an appearance in my school band oddly. We did a parade downtown and somehow we collaborated with Coke Cola of which he worked for and drove the truck during the parade. Now Mom kept in contact with this one man so I'd see him once maybe twice; but the next time I spoke to him I was nineteen. I had heard he opened a major restaurant in Tacoma. I had been looking for part-time work, so I went in with Mom to talk about getting hired. He took me in, but I ended up working one night.

I had just moved in with whom was going to be my husband, and I did all the woman duties by the book. Reported back on threats to the relationship, cooked, cleaned, fucked on schedule, did my best to keep my mouth shut in every outside situation. I told him everting, so he already knew about, he voiced his concerns; but I had already told Mom's old boyfriend I'd be there. After my first night, I reported back, just like any good wife to be should right? Well, not so simple. Old boyfriend was proud to have me there! I was Mom's daughter; I didn't know any other place where this was a good thing. I was introduced as this, "This is her daughter! I dated her mother! And now she's working for me! Anything she needs!" Felt like I was in Good Fellas, and I'm Henry fucking Hill, minus the key bumps. Everyone was great, and this next part was one of the hardest things I didn't have the words to explain. I went home, explained my night and my soon to be husband said, "I don't like that at all, call and let him know you won't be going back." I felt so special there, how was I going to do that? I had history with him; he wasn't going to let anything bad happen to me, what was I doing wrong? But I did it. I protected my inner circle. I cried after making that call, I still don't know what impression that gave him of me for the rest of time, but the family I was building was at stake. Reputation was something I could lose, but loyalty is too important to who I was as a person and what I was about to build with this man.

This was the first of much painful childhood, young adult ties I cut with the blink of an eye to show and secure the unity of family. I've seen that old boyfriend twice since then, the first time after this was aloof with good reason. I expected it and even had an explanation ready. It never made it out, the next was when my brother died.

You see I was requested to be absent at his funeral, but a friend of my brother's and I put together a wake at his gym; and that no one could ask me to leave. My mom's old boyfriend was approached by me and was invited, we were able to share a moment and it was great. The guilt to not being able to explain what happened remains, and I feel an explanation is owed. Background of where I was sitting may shine light on it, but for now the love of old boyfriend in my life was always so innocent. Maybe a tiny part still wishes we got married, wink wink.

The day I met my now ex-husband was the most connected I felt to a family of my own. Something in his eyes told me children, and my best friend, but I knew it when we spoke. There was a hard drive to get pregnant almost immediately, and I thought I didn't want or shouldn't have kids. Looking back, I'm not even sure I had a choice; they were going to be sent to us. I was, at the time, against the grain, and on the fringe of society as much as possible. I had just left high school, got my own apartment by myself down the street from my brother and sister and worked two jobs to ensure not living with anyone continued. I'd frequent to their house for dinners etc. to keep the friendship and brotherhood tight. When I met my ex-husband, we decided to move in together and live thirty minutes in the opposite direction, in an area of town my family never went to but that my ex-husband wanted. I also changed jobs, to something that paid more; then we got pregnant the following year. But it was after we decided to get married. I told my entire family, he told no one. So maybe we weren't getting married, I thought, what's going on? So I made the decision not to get married just because I was having a baby. His family was Catholic, and this didn't go over well; honestly it didn't go over with anyone well.

While I was pregnant I went over and over every detail of my own childhood. Wanted to do everything in my power to shield my baby from all threats and be the mother I never had; so I set out to do so. From the second she was born, no one could touch her. No cursing, no smoking, no drug use, not even unclean hands; she was in a bubble. The slightest intention of evil, I walked her right out. I didn't care who it was; I even did it with my brother and sister a few times just for cursing! Just wanting life to be different for my daughter. I remember this time being particularly difficult for me; I was at odds with everyone. Accused of EVERYTHING under the sun: prude, hypocrite, too good for anyone, denying who I really was; all of it, I heard it. But why was it so fucking wrong I wanted to completely change the environment for this innocent soul? And why are you cowards too weak to do it for your own? I was more than willing to take whatever punishment came my way for her. Not only was it my duty, but responsibility as her mother to pave the way. I was her first coach, and a coach needs to foresee all angles from opposing teams. Interception, and to be able to lead their player to victory.

I remember taking so many backlashes at being hypocritical on "how I'm pretending to be a completely different person." If I was telling my brother and sister who to be in their own house I can go fuck myself! In retrospect, they were right. No one should be able to tell someone what they can or cannot say or do in their own home. But my responsibility to this child meant everything. I was, and still am willing to sacrifice anything for both my children. I had atomic bomb fights for these kids, but not one I'd take back. If I never got to fight for me as a kid, they were both having at least one person that was in their corner no matter what for the rest of my life. I fought against my sister, Mom, Dad, stepmom, my brother from my Dad, my ex-husband's family, and my brother. Any time with my children needed to be supervised through me, no funny business. I would make sure zero attempts at their welfare were being disturbed. If you did spend time the questions in my head would start: why? What are your intentions? What are you doing to her? Are you molesting her?

I watched everyone's eyes, hands, every detail in tones of voice. "She's so beautiful." Okay, that was said awkwardly, look close at that guy.

She got older, walking, talking it got worse. Mom was still talking to the same boyfriend that got funny with me so I was even more helicopter. I couldn't work, because if my ex and I couldn't get opposite shifts there was no such thing as child care in my mind. One we couldn't afford sending my entire paycheck to them, and second me couldn't trust anyone. After finally battling out work schedules, we finally realized me staying home while the kids were young was the only option.

I gave everything of who I was to my husband when we moved in together. The only model of a family I had was from my brother and sister and my nieces being the only children I'd ever been in contact with besides my younger brother. My ex had a younger brother as well and a sister, recently divorced parents of which his dad was about to remarry and have another kid at age fifty. When we met, his parents had barely got divorced and he was twenty and I was just turning nineteen. My ex was interested in me but it came with contingencies. At the time we worked for the same company, and he wouldn't date anyone he worked with. A new job fell into my lap that offered more money, I took it and we started dating. Seven months later we decided to move in together and move on the opposite side of town. My brother didn't like this being far from him and my sister. In general none of our families were really okay with moving thirty minutes by freeway in the opposite direction. We got general shit for living together, which was ironic because everyone around us lived together prior to being married or ever got married at all. We both ended up getting jobs closer to where we lived and we were closer to his family but further from mine. I didn't mind at the time, I just traded one family ridicule for another. I was the only white person in his family of Catholics and I was a bad influence on their eldest son. So not only could I not cook worth a damn, but I was the whipping post of all jokes, nothing I wasn't used to. The best part, not only did I not know the family dynamic to speak too much yet, but he never said anything in my defense! Always just sat back and watched the show; interesting. It wasn't until we would get home from family dinners that I'd unload all of my anger and question our own dynamic as a united front in the world. Nothing changed, except for me, I don't put up with being attacked. I wasn't letting either of us put up with it. I gathered this was always his life there too, and no more was it to continue. I'd been there, and we were going to live differently. Just when I started to pee around us to mark some sort of boundary territory he'd end up calling me out for it in front of everyone in the form of a joke to win points! I was going to be his scape goat at his family's chair? Um, no way. This wasn't a united front; this was betrayal in my book. But simultaneously during this arrival of thought I saw not only myself in him, but I saw my children. It wasn't long before I was pregnant. It wasn't just about him or me anymore, and no one was crossing my child. Period. I'm still this way today, and it's never mattered who it is.

When we told his parents I was pregnant they asked if we were getting married. Now I'd already said we were, but remember, he never "got around to telling his family." So now he had to say, "It'll happen before the baby comes." I said with disgust, "I'm not getting married now just because we are having a baby!" And that went to all family members. I was having second thoughts on marriage at this point due to lack of unity, there was none. And a marriage cannot be built on pebbles, I need poured concrete, earth; not water.

Whispers turned to blathered demands after she was born about getting married. Accusations of me being sac-religious, controlling, out for money, all went around. Then after she was born I didn't want her to be touched, even by doctors! So again I was asked if I was in a cult, psychological issues etc., all were the talk amongst his family. Fun times. To be clear, I just didn't want her hurt, or with anyone I didn't trust; so if you were against me I couldn't trust you. No way in hell am I handing you my new born! I was a nervous wreck when anyone would walk near her, still am. I was determined to give her one person that would kill for her, I never had it. I broke down a lot doing this. The fight with family and the public to be on their best behavior around her was unreal. Every move anyone made wasn't good enough for her, even my ex-husband.

I'd yell when things weren't right, drink to escape the ones I couldn't change (when she got a little older) it's all I knew how to do. Self-medicate the stress away. Finally a breaking point where I couldn't take being alone in the fight anymore I left my ex-husband and moved out with her. I thought we'd just do it alone. That I realized was putting her through an even worse situation, so we reconciled and got pregnant again; it was planned, both children. For nine months during my son's pregnancy all I heard from my ex-husband's dad, "you just got him to take you back because you're pregnant with some other guy's kid and you know he'll pay for it." Then he actually made me apologize to HIM! Not my ex-husband, but to him for the embarrassment I caused his family. Not only like I was his kid, but treating me like I was to begin with. And he asked for it in my house! Finally the day my son was born I requested his dad not be allowed in the room, that was ignored, and I guess his talking did something to my ex-husband because I'll never forget being asked "is he really mine?" Not a chance in hell he wasn't, and hours after giving birth nonetheless.

Now I'm no saint, I've done my share of shitty things. I've had two affairs while being married. Both on the ends of either separating or moving out, or divorce but I did them. I've yelled at my children more than I should have and have scared them. I have drunk excessively, and have gotten angry. To my memory, I have not hit my children out of "just because" moments. They may have different memories; I hope to God I haven't done anything that has deeply hurt them through all my mess. I was in a war in my mind and with everyone around us and on the verge of one nervous breakdown after another. I pulled from any resource to keep sane for them, at all costs.

I'm glad my children have each other, above all each other. It took me about two more years to realize all the promises to be a united front of a family weren't changing. So I'd sit in silence through family functions, drink when I got home, took the shit talk and followed how my ex-husband and his family wanted me to be. Sat in silence at family functions with a smile and nodded with the ridicule of how I wasn't mothering right. Followed my brother and sister how they'd want me to be when I was there. Went to my Dad and stepmom's, shift again, followed that protocol; each location shifting to a new version of a personality to avoid conflict. Who they wanted me to be; even when I was home I couldn't be me there, I started skipping thoughts and opinions of each location including my own to avoid fighting, just did what I thought my husband wanted me to be. He did work a lot, so I was in charge of all things school, play dates, friends, family get together, birthdays, holidays, lunches, dinners, doctors, grocery store, cleaning, bathing, house care. Every night when the kids fell asleep I'd drink myself to a stopper, because I had become everyone's puppet. It was no longer my family, my world, my marriage, or me. It became a picture on a wall of what was expected, and I slowly lost my mind.

I hated my clothes, my hair; I looked in the mirror and didn't know who I was. I changed my wardrobe each week, cut and dyed my hair, tried new makeup; anything to feel something. This "scared" everyone into thinking I was having a mental breakdown, which in a way I was. It put a band aid on how I was feeling; but it didn't cure it. Too much judgement in the eyes of other parents, family members, put me right back to pulling out my old clothes and growing out my hair, so I ran instead. Oppression and evil works by constricting, surrounding and pushing inward. I'm still in this today; there are sections in my closet of where I will be going that day. There is no me, honestly, I have no clue what that person looks like on the outside. I have a clear picture on the inside, yet to the world it has to be masked per location; right down to the hair choice. It's very calculated to the audience, and effective. If you want a certain reaction, you will get it based on appearance I've learned. So I use it. There is no sense of self, just based on appearance. It's all reaction.

I always had a hard time in school. I worked ten times harder than my peers at what seemed easy for them, and cried during the more difficult. When I'd ask for help at home, Dad gave a few minutes and gave up. Grandpa would help the longest but then would get frustrated I still didn't get it. Dad and grandmother would tell me I was just stupid, and it would look bad if we had a retarded member in our family. I'd cry in class a lot if I didn't get a perfect score. But I never was tested for any delays, special needs, or disabilities. How would that look right? I literally could not remember anything or understand book work. Then I was scared to death not getting it would mean at home, so getting straight A's I made happen up to seventh grade. Cheating, manipulating teachers or any way I could was a priority. When a child is in fight, flight, or freeze mode they can't learn a new skill; now that's proven. How long have I been there? Birth to present I'm guessing, but I'm no professional. I'm just amazed some days I can still wipe my own ass. Then seventh grade; an alarm went off. When it did everything came crashing down; and looking back I wonder what my life could have been if this one alarm hadn't gone off. College perhaps, the dreams I did have for myself as far as school and my future. School, curriculum never made sense to me; I never remember what I read for starters so that dream was a bust from the get go. I can't function at a job, so thanks a lot Mrs. G for shinning that light on my reality.

I was sitting in health class during the first session I've ever had of abuse. The differences on each one, what they may look like and how to spot them; I remember tearing up. Some believe emotional abuse can be more damaging than physical abuse. I used to literally pray to be hit rather than go through the torment grandmother and Dad put me through, so honestly I have not the two to compare but I did think it would have been quicker. Mine was drawn out, over hours and years. I'd even ask grandmother, "Can you just hit me and leave instead?" Nope. I wish she would have, it would have saved time. Dad's drink of choice was intimidation and scare tactics, which was a nice change.

I had a Barbie dream house as a Christmas gift when my folks where still married, so age 3-5. Came with a ton of Barbie's and their dishes, furniture and I had their little cars even. I loved it so much, and Dad and I'd play a lot. We were also into movies, old black and whites. Marcs Bros., W.C. Fields "It's a Gift," "Psyco," "Halloween." Everyone is familiar with Michael Myers from that last movie by this point. Dad decided it would be fun to stage my Barbie house like a movie. So when I went to play again, well, everyone was dead. Ken was masked and in all black just as the character in the movie, propped up standing in the Barbie house with a little knife tapped to his little hand. All the other Barbie's were naked with blood drawn all over them; dead. He's laughing, I'm crying. He kept this "prank" going for several years. I was older; we had moved out of my grandma's house and went on our own. One night I was asleep and the theme song to Halloween started blaring from the living room. I ran in, and he's standing in the middle with a sheet over himself and glasses. If any of you have seen the very first movie, there is a scene where the character does this. Says nothing; and still to this day I can't hear that theme song or see that mask without a slight reaction. And yet another example, one night I wanted to take a shower before we watched another movie. He said, "No, do it after trust me."

It was fucking Psyco! Then I have to shower just after watching it; and he has the gulf to walk in during me shampooing. Just a breeze by to intensify the movie for me; thanks Dad. But seriously, thank you, you were the first of many to teach me fear is an illusion of distraction. It's also a valuable tool to survival. So from the bottom of my heart thank you, I fear very little now; and what I do fear I know exactly what to do with it. I'm very glad you were given to me to teach me hard core lessons I wouldn't have learned any other way. Control, sadism, thief, S&M, fear, manipulation, reaction, human behavior, social class, self-mutilation, carnage, the dark parts of me that I even enjoy at times; that was all you. That's your DNA; yours and grandmothers. I'm a better person for it, simply because I choose to navigate it. Never suppressing it because you'll have an implosion or explosion; can't deny who you are, even if there are parts that aren't pretty to others.

Dad ignored everything grandmother did, I told him about all of it thinking he'd rescue me, it did nothing. She still had to babysit me when he worked. Much to my surprise everything I said was being told to her anyway. I told him she drove her car up onto curbs when she got mad at my mom and was yelling at me over it; holding knives to my face when I walked home from the bus at her house. No changes were made, it just continued. I even told Mom and nothing stopped, I was still put back in that house.

Dad never valued me as a person, I was different than him in opinion, values, thoughts etc., and it wasn't tolerated. If it wasn't seen or done his way it was ridiculed; then silenced. That was after being severely yelled at for being different than him; if he was white and you were black on a subject get ready for it! Then you'd be cast away. Then I'd go to Mom's where there was no yelling, no scolding, no ridicule, no interaction, nothing; I was alone. I sat in the living room of a two bedroom apartment while she and her boyfriend where closed in one room, his son closed in the other. Silence. The occasional contact high would drift out or someone would try to catch me in the shower but that was it. No one to see if I got to school, no one checking my meals or hygiene or mental state. Just there, I was thirteen. Didn't she miss me all this time? Wasn't she concerned about how I'd been or what I'd been through? How I was getting to school or who my friends would be at this new school I now had to go to in her district? All of my things were in a garbage bag, was she going to help me unpack? Do I put it in the kitchen?

Do you know what was of concern? What she would make time for? If I was available to talk about her boyfriend and her relationship; his kids, their mother. What if he was cheating on her? Where he worked, if he was home on time, where he was? Let's drive and spy on him, look through his pockets. We even drove and I took a huge rock and smashed a possible woman he'd been cheating on her with through her windshield for her one night. Those were the only times I got to "bond" with my mother, and still; it was about her. Helping her with her problems or listening to her issues and helping her work through them. If she'd be able to make rent, buy cigarettes or afford food. I had to figure out if she got the child support that month or if she had a job, there was no time for school work. I was the rescuer, she never took the advice, but if I wanted her time it needed to be about her. If the conversation took a turn to me or anyone else in any shape of form it was over or she'd get pissed. Still to this day, if I have a burden of any kind she doesn't want to hear it; that's my problem to deal with; I'm here to help her, period.

We moved four to six more times before my senior year because of either evictions or breakups, and at times we needed to pack and move while the guy was at work that day and finally I saved enough money to buy my own car cash while working after school or on weekends with the help of my brother and sister taking me to look at some cars. Took me another few months later to get a one bedroom apartment down the street from them on my own. I went to night school two years, and two years of summer school to be able not to graduate with my own class.

I never got to walk, wear a cap and gown or hear my name called. I was molested or raped (depending on how you view it) for over a year by one of the basketball coaches at my high school. I ended up going back later and telling the principal after my daughter was born; he let me take my missing credits for my diploma. The teacher was fired but ended up going to another school to teach shortly after, justice never seems to happen.

I did work two jobs, bought my own car and had my own place to breathe at eighteen; for a while anyway.

Why am I almost forty still talking about my parents' divorce when I was five years old and everything in detail after that? Why can't I let anything go you possibly are asking right? Great questions and they both have to do with "clinical" answers I'm sure; like fight or flight, and trust amongst others. As I've grown and had other relationships even potentially healthy ones didn't stand a chance because of the inner monologue that runs as a broken record in place to remind me not to let those things happen again. It's not even not being able to move on from instances, but rather remembering as a kid when you touch fire you get burned; and where all the matches are kept. The list of where matches are kept are just so detailed, it's down to every manufacturers eight hundred number in case of an emergency! You become a prisoner of your own making, and it does get lonely, or is it? I'll get to that.

There were brief moments in my life of living alone that I felt free. I could feel who I was; find out who that was fully. The only time It didn't infringe on anyone's beliefs, way of life, how I was supposed to be, how I was supposed to eat, when I could sleep, when I could pray, how I wanted to pray, how I spoke, how I dressed, wore makeup, felt, or expressed feelings.

This MASS control on every fuck move, every decision, every word choice I've ever made is never ending; the silencing of it all. The mistrust in every idea or choice I've tried to make is always wrong! It fuels anger. Zero freedom of mind, body, career, and family; it's controlled. What's the icing on the cake? They laugh while they know they're in the position of authority to control me. Just recently in fact I've developed a tick. Not a real one you get in the woods, but an actual crazy person physical response. I used to make fun of these all the time in people, I fully understand them now. I'll shiver, just like it's too cold outside. Full body, all of it; and not much else besides time helps it. I have zero vises, although dying to know why DMT isn't legal and the drug that kept my mother in the arms of a man rather than mothering is now; blows my mind. Now I shake? I LOVE how marijuana is the worst drug to hide, yet denial was the way to go with mom for years. Did it in front of me on the trip for me to get molested with her boyfriend's brother, but nope, that wasn't her I saw? Denial? It's actually called gas-lighting.

Now I just shake. I literally cannot logically understand a person without balls. Gas lighting has to be at the top of my list as the most infuriating things a person can do. Simply admit it, accept the responsibility and move on. It takes a bigger man to admit a sin and punishment, than to shrink in the corner. Even bigger man to stand in a crowd and admit it during the stone toss, all while explaining he did it for the greater good of mankind.

I was about twelve when a friend of mine thought a sleep over with the Ouija board was a good idea. I had already seen the Exorcist a few times and knew of this "game." After playing for a short time she got tired and laid down on the floor, only to abruptly sit up again against the wall. This would be my first encounter with an attachment/possession in my life face to face.

Parts of her were there but weren't, so looking back and if I had to guess it may have been just channeling, but this being and I spoke until sunrise. What I'll never forget is what it looked like. It wasn't until I got older and the internet became more advanced that I was able to piece it together. I was able to get a clearer picture of the being when I slightly looked away, out of my peripheral vision. The body was extremely gargoyle yet tall; very long arms and legs. Fingers and feet were in human comparison large. The face and head, big surprise was goat-like. Yes, nothing new here except possibly for the color; green. I would get scared I saw it, flick my eyes back up at my friend, and her mouth would barely smile. For what had to be over four hours because we started playing at around midnight until the sun rose, she didn't move once. Arms up over her knees bent to chest up against the wall just a few word answer sentences and slow blinks. The sun was coming up, and finally it slumped over to a laying position and closed her eyes. The next morning she had no memory after a few questions of the game and the rest I kept to myself. Her life took a major nose dive of violence and poverty; needless to say we parted ways. But to this day I'll never forget the few words spoken in a time jump of hours that seemed like minutes.

The next year when I was living at moms, I woke in the middle of the night to which I thought was her boyfriend laying behind me in the spooning position. I was frozen in fear, not knowing if I should scream or run. I started crying and shaking thinking this was the moment I get raped. I slowly moved my shin over my left shoulder to even more fear; just a black mass. At the same time I screamed at what I saw it spun me like a clock in the bed. Just then I seemed to wake up as if I'd dreamed the entire thing, although I knew I had not. My heart racing I checked for any evidence and the only thing I had were a few scratches and bruises. I told mom about the bruises and scratches and all she said was it wasn't good, but no help. Different variations of this went on for the next year.

I love it when a therapist or friend asks me if I was ever sexually abused growing up, I think to myself, "You have no idea."

I was raped by an ex-boyfriend in high school and called police with a girl friend of mine and did a report at her apartment (she was two years older) and not one thing was done. I went home to then tell my sister and no reaction. Which made me think of the time she was assaulted when she was in high school in a parking lot, I was still young. She came home and told mom and I a guy came up to her and rubbed his "juices" on her lip and left. Mom called the police, they came out did a report and we took my sister to get checked out at the doctor to make sure she was ok. My sister knew of the rape in high school, the teacher, told my brother and mom both I think. Dad then knew the rape, unsure if he knew of the teacher but that was it; they just knew. His response, "I told you not to date a black man." My sister is mom's daughter too, so I have a feeling what I told her, mom knew about most of it; but I was just there.

It is the best joke in the world to me when a new person in my life says these words: you need to learn to trust people, or why is loyalty so huge with you? Or my favorite, why can't you give anyone a chance?

Seriously? I've been a pawn in everyone's chess game for utter amusement I'm guessing. Not giving a shit for what happens to a life after creating it is reckless. Ill deal with how I handle the aftermath, I don't need how anyone perceives it.

COMPASS

--- ✦◆✦◆✦◆✦ ---

"Forget the politicians. The politicians are put there to give you the idea that you have freedom of choice. You don't. You have no choice. You have owners, they own you. They own everything, they own all the important land, and they own and control the corporations. They've long bought and paid for the Senate, the Congress, the State houses, the city halls, they've got the judges in their back pockets. And they own all the big media companies so they control all of the news and information you get to hear. They got you by the balls! It's a big club, and you aint in it; you and I are not in the big club. By the way it's the same big club they use to beat you over the head with all day long when they tell you what to believe. All day long in their media, what to believe and what to think and what to buy. The table is tilted folks, the game is rigged. And nobody seems to notice, nobody seems to care. Good honest hard working people; blue collar, white collar doesn't matter what color shirt you have on. Good honest hard working people continue, these are people of modest means, continue to elect rich cock suckers who don't give a fuck about them! They don't care about you at all. No one seems to notice, no one seems to care. That's what the owner seems to count on, that Americans will probably remain willfully ignorant. Because the owners of this country know the truth; it's called: the American Dream. Because you have to be asleep to believe it."

~G. Carlin

Do an experiment; draw a triangle on a piece of paper fairly large so
you can label it. now divide it into thirds where the bottom has the
most space, the center having less than the bottom, and finally the
top of the pyramid the least amount of space; we're going to label
this, so keep it by you.

The total population currently is 7.8 billion people in the world.
There are 2,604 billionaires alive today so write this number at the
top of your pyramid. The next is 46.8 million millionaires living
today, this goes in the center of your drawing. Finally on the bottom is this number: 7,753,197,396. That is everyone else that isn't
in those brackets. That's how many people who are not elite. This is
important on what I'm about to tell you that you already know, so
stay with me.

Money as we all know equals power, control and influence. How
far has/does this evil eye go? These people are exclusive not only to
themselves but to the rest of society. Why wouldn't they be right? In
business, school, law, finance etc. At the same time it's a hierarchy
to the rest of influence of absolutely anything that comes to mind.
Could it be for amusement, a greater plan? Well, if you're awake,
look and see the clues.

Everything sinister is veiled with a story of doing well. It must
have someone behind the scenes pumping out a "microchip the
infant" campaign with Sarah McLaughlin holding a one eyed dog.
Somehow it feels like you're doing something right because a celebrity is doing it. Think, they're in one of the top tiers, they're and
influencer of the masses. Take covid-19, first a panic to get everyone
scared (scare tactics are very effective when moving large numbers
of people) then enclosurement, then take away basic human needs,

keep them there for as long as we can and whoever doesn't kill each other will agree to whatever we say willingly. No matter what it is? Take them down to animals first, slaves to us first, and then they will obey. While they're hidden in their homes, we can get out and move mass amounts of our shit they couldn't see. They won't ask questions right now because everything is closed. They can freely charge and infuse places, items and medicine as they see fit without anyone being aware or questioning it. Why? Because we crave safety? We know how to self-preservation, there should be no panic or fear; or most important no dependency on another avatar holding that compass. I understand disease and death happens, and everyone should do their part in helping others. I'm a big advocate of prevention, yet acceptance on what is; what's in front of you was meant to be. Not to run from anything. I'll say it until I'm blue in the face, plants are our only medicine!

Think about that picture you made often, I do for many symbolic reasons. First, it's a pyramid, there are three points; but then because the majority of the population obeys because of power and money and that fact angers me to no end. There's a lot to know with the number three, there's good and bad in it, but I did tell you to put it into that so take from it what you will.

Let me breakdown numbers for you, and open your eyes to the clues you were given here that are in everything all around you. Symbols are in everything telling you what you need to know without asking.

Zero: Unity, never ending, absolution

One: Godly, selfish

Two: simple, dual nature, balance

Three: trinity, good relationships, wealth

Four: unconventional, wholeness, cross, burden, suffer, change

Five: intellect, sex, determination, incomplete house

Six: love, intellect, marriage, mark

Seven: luck, complete home, determination, victory, ruler

Eight: evolution, infinity, time travel, time continuum

Nine: war, aggression, confusion, sympathy, empathy

These numbers are single digits with their meaning and must be identified as such. Meaning, if you have a larger than a single digit it then must be added together until you come up with a single number; this is your answer. Where are they? Everywhere. From when you were born to the house you live in, to your social security and phone number. These are not accidents, and they are clues to everything. Why are there Angels assigned to each minute of time to this dimension? There's a reason for it and that number has a code; but there is always two codes to decipher. What is above is also below and usually going on sideways as well.

When the frequency, or vibration in the world is raised after fear and segregation are achieved; of which is strategically manipulated by the elite, fortunately the rest of the population I hope is pushed into this forced "harvest time." Granted it is set up this way by the elite for their plans, yet being the majority we should use it to our advantage. We are able to tap into an evolutionary consciousness not normally reached under normal circumstances. The catch here is to be able to do it just as the elite do it to us; in secret. No protesting in the streets, no Instagram stories, nothing that shows we know any of their plans. We "mimic" their behavior, meet in secret and "harvest" our awakening. The more we become aware, the less we can become controlled. No mass hysteria, a unified consciousness of calm consensus on how to overturn a revolution; or how to make it out alive. Take the harvest time to learn and feel discernment to be able to move forward, be aware of the bandwagon of propaganda. Stay calm and cautious of instant changes. Remembering just like with oppression and possession it's a slow power build. If anyone says anything is happening immediately it's usually a scare tactic to something insidious underlying.

Operation Paperclip was a classified military program with a public persona. German troops and scientist in facilities with "good guy" faces in or at the end of World War 2. Not discounting all sixteen hundred of these people, I'd like to think there was at least one infiltrator amongst them trying to overturn this. In short, U.S. intelligence program brought Nazi German scientists to U.S. soil to then "harness their brain power" for cold war initiatives. The goal was to use the Germans to develop our rockets and biological and chemical weapons; all the while not letting it get into the hands of the Soviet Union. Truman was behind this although didn't want to recruit Nazi's. However JIOA, OSS, and the CIA did it anyway and scrubbed any evidence that it had been done; or so they thought. This is all information available and I urge you to put this down and look it up for yourself. In one ledger written between the scientists, it reads: of the hundred prisoners you sent, they died during transport. Please send more. Yet the assignment was for rockets?

I'm bringing this up for the reason of symbology, and numerology; because it's our map. The elite and the underbelly of government are sinister but never fail to rear its infused symbology throughout history.

Really look at the number five, there's even a movie dedicated to it yet "they" discredited it widely as a flop and named it the Number 23. Now yes the movie in its storyline was a bit lacking, but the number is very real. Two plus three equals five, five in history is repeated in a LOT of horrific events just as the movie explains:

The alphabet – 23 letters = 5

Hiroshima – 8-6-1945 = 23 =5

King Charles I – had 23 Knights Templar = 5

Witches Sabbath – 6-23

Shakespeare born and dies April 23 = 5

Titanic sank April 15 1912 = 23 = 5

TWA flight 800 – 230 died. Explosions in seats 23J and 23k = 5

Caesar stabbed 23x = 5

Charles Manson born 11-12-1934 = 23 = 5

9-11-2001 = 23 = 5

Illuminati 23a.d. = 5

UFO sightings are the highest on July 23 = 5

Do a visualization experiment for this, draw on a piece of paper a star. Label off to the side: Earth, Air, Fire, Water, and Spirit. Then draw, to the best of your abilities, a stick figure person. Looks like the star yes? Head, two arms, two legs and a center right? This is what not only the star, but the number five represents in symbology. Di Vinci knew this in his representation of the Vitruvian Man. Now, as with everything, turn your paper upside down. What do you see? Perhaps a pentagram in opposition? Exactly. Looking at the number five a bit differently with the dates above now?

World War I began and ended both with the number five. Operation Paperclip began with the number one (selfish), ended with the number five. U.S. declared war on Germany 12-11-1941, five; Hitler's suicide, the Declaration of Independence!

Numbers that are on repeat: five, four, six nine. Why? Because of what they stand for, it's not a coincidence. Those are your clues, use them.

What number do you see on the Nazi symbol four times? Right. Do you think this was an accident? What is four and seven? Eleven and two is dual nature. But a four is burden, suffering. A seven is determination and victory; the symbol is placed as a repelling blade! Think about it, and then think about what happened. Do you know who came up with the term conspiracy theorists first? The CIA, not the patrons drawing conclusions from facts. Not people having experiences and writing about them or putting these horrid acts in history on blast. It's a scare tactic title given by the CIA! The elite, as a hush order. They did it to Snowden, and nothing he reported was false. Yet the majority of the population choses to believe the minority because they are our masters?! No thanks.

After Project Paperclip two of those "doctors" then went to Camp King; take a guess what its nickname was? "The Goat Farm." I'm not making this shit up. It was agricultural at the start, then used for interrogation. In Frankfurt, Germany far from U.S. laws and out of sight, this "black sight" is where the most horrific testing on human subjects; MK Ultra.

If your new to MK Ultra, it's the use of psychedelic drugs, paralytics and electroshock therapy all the while under hallucinogens being bombarded with information; sexual and physical abuse. Think of the movie: A Clockwork Orange. Drugs used include: MDMA, mescaline, heroin, barbiturates, methamphetamine, and psilocybin. Operation Midnight Climax was a sub-project under MK Ultra where prostitutes were taken and experimented on mostly in San Francisco and New York. Ken Kesey, the author of the 1962 One Flew Over the Cuckoo's Nest, VOLUNTEERED for MK Ultra while he was at Stanford. So this shows it was most definitely on U.S. soil by the 1960s.

During the "brainwash" period under hallucination, frequency and or vibration is added as a tone to activate or de-activate a subject. Repeatedly flashes of image, sounds over and over, symbols. Now think to current day, what's changed? Nothing if you ask me. Where has the elite put our drugs? EVERYWHERE, it's just been in small doses. Fluoride, pesticides, pharmaceuticals, creams, cleaning supplies, vaccinations, yearly vaccinations. While "programming" (look for that word everywhere) what they want you to view on the T.V., in the movies, on the radio. The same sounds, over and over again. Let's employ Steve fucking Jobs to do the job. The activation to turn off their immune systems can be the announcement of 5G. Give 'em all some toys to play with like fucking toddlers. Right before flu that we can call a pandemic or make it one by paying our doctors under the table to falsely diagnose any illness to say it's the flu to increase the numbers. If we play it right, they'll be so fucking dependent on our vaccine we can put what we need them to take in it. Genius.

But not really if your awake, if you can see the plan. Just because you are being recorded and monitored in your home because you chose to be, doesn't mean you can't make another choice. Just because they can now control the atmosphere with HAARP, doesn't mean you don't ride out that storm!

The goal is always power and control, anyway possible, and trust me its anyway possible. MK Ultra was/is to control people, HAARP the environment, CIA and politicians run it all. What wasn't accomplished or can't be by either will be by Hanson robotics and Apple. Which symbolically the devil himself held to Eve in Genesis. I swear, it's like everyone is asleep and thinks it's funny when I point out the blatant mocking that is today.

But I'm just crazy right? Just have a mental illness that needs to be medicated right?

If you think these people don't belong to the same bowling league, think again. There's a pentagram of blood that runs over and along major cities all over the world. How many points to a pentagram? Five. Think about it.

A one nation, a unified people, new world order, one way, is simply the story of the Tower of Babel. We have been diversified and set on separate paths for a reason, to enrich and learn from one another. Not to conform, not to be enslaved, certainly not to go back to cattle. I ask, why are we allowing it? Why are we dismissing obvious signs and not taking a stand? I have, am I alone?

Now if you haven't noticed there's a lot here that's in opposition, mainly because I don't have all the answers. None of us do I don't think, but you'll see I've even noticed I've said, "Take a stand, yet mimic their behavior and stay quiet." However they haven't stayed quiet truly, it's all over the fucking T.V., and all throughout history. So to tell you the truth, I don't know the exact tactic that would work to our advantage the best. I can only lay out the madness perhaps. Or perhaps somehow doing both would be the best art of war. Try to seek out the number seven and one as much as you can, is cautious of terms that veil underlying agendas.

I lost my seven in this realm, so I am left with my four. I will forever feel "missing a piece" so to speak. But he was here with me writing every word of this, and for that I am thankful. Just as he will and is talking to me each day. Even though my avatar can't seem to understand that concept no matter how hard I push it to the limits. It's not capable, so I just accept that.

Accepting conformity in this realm isn't something I'm willing to do, never could, and I'm not fucking bred for it. Simply put, my spirit isn't about another agenda; it's about a higher one just one. I fight for that, without fail; mistakes yes, but without fail.

So if you're asking me how do we fight back, overturn this hell on earth; me? It's heavy, its broad, its engrained so deep and wide I'm honestly not sure the best line of fire. By what I know, we have not the financial capabilities, military, courts, environment, technology, media, or agriculture. So what's left? Maybe, just maybe, in the numbers; I can hope I am not alone in spirit. That within the 7,753,197,396 people it's not all just drones; but I've already done the math and it's not promising. The first picture I had you draw, when you combine the billionaires and the millionaires it equals the number three, mocking of the holy trinity; or illuminati if you really want to take it further. Take a wild guess what adding up the rest of the population comes to, five. The chess game is fixed, and it's not in our favor. All I can feel is off grid, but would you do it? Would you sacrifice all your luxuries for the greater good for who you were bred to work for? I know I would give the chance; it's all I've ever wanted. Let's test that theory; let's see how many of you would give up luxury, false security, technology, media, forced to culture your own food again because it's close to what it's come to for a pure existence. Purity in the form of oneself, away from these veiled words: entertain, Hollywood, channels, programming, followers, media, technology, bio-poisoning, pharmaceuticals. I agree, slavery isn't over; because people choose to be slaves. Volunteer for programming everyday as if the 60s never ended. It's a choice still, let's not make it forced; maybe we still have that option. Maybe that's our only card here to play, we have the numbers to create a "no more volunteers" we choose nothing over bullshit.

There always seems to be this mass round up of the on the fringe radicals of individuals that don't go with the flow or are out of the norm of society. It's ok if society changes, but not if a small group or individual changes for himself or God forbid the greater good. Not to mention should that come as a threat to local police or military. A right to bear arms and freedom of thought and speech, religion out on your own; not on paper, but is a felony, if caught death. If the elite feels particularly amused with you and can see an opportunity for career advancement and/or currency off your right to be human, then it's dragged out. You're mocked, tagged, splashed all over the news and paraded like a circus animal until all currency is drained after everyone has seen the show. The sick part is we go to see that show! We can all do something about it by simply refusing to buy the damn tickets. The tickets are sold in every newspaper, every media story, even school are selling it. There's a fine line between history and individuals being taken advantage of. Sold after very simply refusing to abide by a forced interpretation of their reality that hurts no one. An individual, out on their own living how they choose not hurting or infringing on any other individual and let's toss in a registered legal weapon just for argument. This person shouldn't be bothered by anyone as long as they're doing the same right? So why are they? Notice how when a group of like-minded of the same, gathering with him/her it's when the elite get nervous. Police are called, "we have a situation." But did we? What if, before the police, military, cameras and media show up and spin it for your tickets to the show it was a simple story?

Simply people among the 7,753,197,396 that are becoming aware? Attempting to refuse dosing, grab their gun and head out into a cabin. Fuck what if, we are prosecuting our group? Trying to make a run for it and no one is listening. Because the story we get is what?

Radicals, crazy, or horrific stories of cults. I'm not saying these stories aren't gut wrenching, but are they meant to be to get us to be scared? Did you know David Koresh's birthday is 8-17-1959, which adds down to 22, of course is a four? His message needed to be through suffering and burden. If you look at the number four as a cross, even the crucifix as the symbol of the ultimate sacrifice, then think of how he lived and his message. It was pure, regardless of how the outside would or you and I view it. To him, he was on mission; he meant what he said whole heartedly and his existence was going to see that through. That was his path from his creator given to him, if others had similar paths, why was there military involvement to that extent? I'm simply talking of just those points; if children are being hurt, anyone is being held anywhere against their will, stolen weapons, or pedophilia of any kind is punishable. Agreed. Take those facts out, if they were even there in the first place honestly, and dissect what happened with the Davidians chronologically and by numbers.

The date the standoff began was on 2-28-1993 = adding down to a 7

The date it ended was on 4-19-1993 = adding down to a 1

What does that tell you? I know what it says to me. It says it started as a victorious determination of his idea of a complete house. It ended selfishly and on God's terms. So fuck, none of us were there for the most part so that's all we can go on. All the while Jeffrey Epstein, Marina Abramović, James Gunn out shaking hands with presidents and celebrities right out in front of your faces or posting on social media with no military intervention?! What am I missing? Is it truly sinister, is it a mocking of the trinity, or are some real enlightened beings trying to do the right thing and something gets a hold of it along the way and flips it? Turns it into something dark, and opportunity to stomp out any attempts to fight back? The sad truth is you only know your chart. Beware of anyone trying to change it. Judgement to it from the outside is a test of your strength to stand up against a crowd. Or completely walk the other direction despite the mob is footing it to the hills. Time alone enriches you back to what you already know your truth. But be careful, three days in solitude with no light is an invitation…

PSEUDOSCIENCE

Next, I'm accused over and over of not either knowing how to have relationships, or splitting. If you're not familiar with this term, its okay, I wasn't either until accused. It's clinical for all or nothing thinking; I call it simply my personality! Positive and negative qualities of the self to others into a cohesive, realistic whole. Some could agree it is a defense mechanism, or base it on flight response. Having read the previous chapter, I look at this as "I have no time for bullshit!" I am on borrowed, limited time here, so is everyone else. I have a low, maybe in the negative numbers even, threshold for wasting time. Be clear, to the point and honest when dealing with me. You'll get the same, it will be brief, and we can both move on. Plain and simple. Somehow this is a major fucking issue for 99% of humans, I don't know why. I'm baffled why we can't simply enrich and move on. Support, move forward. Love, share it. Why does everyone want to get muddy? Yet I need to work on my people skills?! How about when everyone goes outside, they can just be ready? Meaning, on point at work, thinking, prepared? I am, I teach my children to be. The moment you hit that door, be fucking ready. Have answers, have all your paperwork ready to go, all of it. Label things, make notes, stay on top of everything. Nothing should catch you off guard, why? Because you went over every angle already, and have an answer or reaction for it. I'll admit it pisses me off when people are not prepared. More to that, when I'm paying them for a service. Even worse, if I'm giving my time in any relationship, and their part is shit. In my head I'm literally questioning why I left the house. The brain dead factor mixed with zero passion drives me up a wall! I blame the city I live in mostly, but maybe my gene pool too. My patience is thin as melting ice on a good day, however, there are two spirits I have been chosen to teach. My children. They are close to me. As close as anyone ever will be. There is nothing that gives me more peace, makes me more alive and full of purpose; knowing that soul contract is obligated to teach them everything I can. To ensure their longevity in spirit. Navigating their avatars, feed their minds and bodies. What they do with the information is of course on them, but it's up to me to show them the worlds. I made that promise, and to them I'm loyal as fuck. I've never felt any other emotion when loyalty to my children for a higher purpose comes into play. Not of shame, taboos, you name it. I'm about them, and my path. I could care less who that makes uncomfortable.

Even when I've tried to simply quit, or get therapy to find ways to; it doesn't take. Panic sets in, I feel unprotected and vulnerable. The pendulum will swing far back in reverse in reclusion. I do know one thing, validation and justification are huge points. Someone with BPD and/or PTSD/CPTSD rarely get validation or justification. If anything, those are two things we get robbed of at every turn, in every sentence, by everyone we encounter. That adds to the second hand clock tick we hear in our heads, or perhaps just my own.

Nuts and bolts of BPD:

Instability of interpersonal relationships

Either love em or hate em

They feel everything

Struggle with self-image

Impulsive, abandonment, emptiness, dissociative symptoms

Genetics in the first degree make it ten times more likely it will pass on

Environment can mold it

Another factor and this is just my theory, can cysts, tumors or concussion play roles? Let's say a patient has a hydrophallus arachnoid cyst at the base of their brain; or location X. Making the surrounding tissue pinched, pushing up against….hypothalamus and the hippocampus? BPD has proven irregularities in the brain, yes? Amygdala that regulated anger, prefrontal cortex for decision making. Hippocampus and hypothalamus sending signals to amygdala; then hypothalamus and hippocampus, regulating bogy function and memory.

Human's prefrontal cortex isn't developed until age twenty five, the longest time a mammal takes to figure shit out. But that's scary at the same time. To all parents out there, children need guidance and protection a lot longer than we originally thought! Now knowing the brain and if signs of these are showing up, it could just be more than environmental, it could be system related. The part that pisses me off is how this isn't categorized as a legit disability! But at the same time how disabilities are viewed anyway. If you have a patient with BPD, due to a cyst, concussion of the brain causing irregularities in memory, anger, decision making, and body function, do you as a society want those individuals serving you as nurses? As teachers to your children? Think about that. Police officers? Stick it into any job field, are you comfortable? Yet at the same time we can't discriminate right? But we do, because no one hires that profile due to what I just said; it's too risky. It's just not said. That same person can't get on disability because they aren't qualified. Where does that leave that population? Swallowing pills to make the rest of you "comfortable?" That sounds like some new world order bullshit to me! Even those who finally give in to that absurd way of thinking to bow to the masses, they've been out of work so long how are we to explain it? Fix it America, Land of the Great, it's a problem.

Myers Briggs has sixteen "personality types" and one of the rarest is INFJ. Making up only about 2% of the entire word's population; and here I am, in another "category." Yet the correlation between INFJs and BPD are eerily similar, just as let's say a person "traveling" from another dimension? Expand your mind; you're only using a small part of it anyway; try imagining what I'm suggesting. Some things are real whether you believe or not. INFJs, meaning: introversion, intuition, feeling and judgement. The characteristics include: mysterious, emotionally intelligent, and referred to as counselor or advocate. They're on a different wavelength (or are they?), their dominant function is intuition and conscientiously notice patterns in everything. Remember what I said there in dimensions, if one can be aware of patterns, one can move within them; hence a higher dimension.

Psychotic-like symptoms and enlightenment look oddly similar, so where is the line between science and God? The forever question right? What are the signs for schizophrenia? In physiology, the DSM5 is used for assessing mental disorders but a diagnosis needs to be made beforehand. How do the "professionals" do this? This specific illness is then looked for with these tell-tell signs. Psychosis is witnessed, where thoughts and feelings are damaged to the point where one has lost all touch with reality. This person will start to experience hallucinations; you mind hearing things, seeing things, and feeling things that aren't really there to the objective world. Or even tactile hallucinations where this person can even feel touching as if another person was going it. Delusion is separate from hallucination whereas it's a firm fixed belief of something that is not possible. Not to be confused with subjective opinions, grandiose delusions, or persecurtory delusions. Episodes of psychosis can last anywhere from an hour to life long. The next thing witnessed is disorganized thinking, it's not logical. Then of course withdrawn or unresent, unsocial. Believe it or not a "professional" will most likely diagnose if you have at least two out of those four for a length of a month! Call me crazy, but a person goes through all of these steps if they're sensitive to a spirit world!

If a hallucination is an uncontrolled perception and perception is a controlled hallucination, then everything is a hallucination. The only difference is consensus; a mass agreeing calling it reality. But perception in the brain is a guess anyway, the world around us and self or the inner movie. Take that with the five senses and collectively us as organisms make up a consciousness. It is only when one consciousness agrees with another we trust it's real. Why? And more importantly, why discount when it is not?

Has a psychologist ever met a medium or a shaman? Probably right, or an exorcist? Not sure how many of those seek therapy, or medicine men, witches or what Marie Laveau's mental state was in?! Do they have any idea what those folks are going through? Is it a mental illness or what an individual is capable of over another? By definition a hallucination is a sense that isn't real; by whose perspective? There are eleven dimensions, and just because one avatar can't see it am I to believe it's not real? Can anyone see the internet? Steve Jobs was celebrated though right? The anti-Christ himself and everyone was along for the ride. When it profits for everyone its somehow ok then yes? If Musk can make something I can touch, I'm ok with his delusions. But if I can't fathom it, I can't touch or buy it, or experience it, it's a "mental illness" is that what we're doing?

One avatar knows nothing "over" another in terms of right and wrong. Only these are the eyes and gifts I was given to use. Each on can enrich the other, not dictate or control thy paths. If you're simply uncomfortable, step aside. The rights of your speck of this dimension should not be force fed down everyone's throat with pharmaceuticals! Some of us were brought here to open your eyes, expand your universe and show everyone what potential we all have. This human experience is brief in an immortal beings' existence. If there are those who truly want to rise up against evil, I challenge you to see how engrained in everything it really is; hush orders on every expansion. Socially in 2016 is when acceptance for all became dominant right? But did it, have you noticed how many rules that came with? A hush order, that's not expansion if there's no freedom. I understand movements take time, we as a people can't seem not to see color and it's been since 1865 since slavery ended in this country. One hundred and fifty five years and for some reason no one has been to therapy. It's like the whole country is dealing with family counseling every day. There's not one person who doesn't agree what happened wasn't punishable, but I do think it isn't present. What was learned is taken and used, but reliving what was not creates invoking what was. Learn from pain and stress, there is no moving through this avatar experience without thanking both the good and the fucking horrific as tools. They all are; it gives us what we need. To burden another avatar is unproductive; enrich, show maps, clues, a flashlight, a mirror, a compass.

Declassified UFOs by the Pentagon during a global pandemic of 2020, as if that number can't harbor enough suffering; why now? One word answer, misdirection. ET, UFOs, MKUltra, eleven dimensions are not unknown, in fact documented. Yet otherwise these individuals have been either killed off, hushed, ran off or deemed "conspiracy theorists" by the CIA themselves. Yes the men in black, I'll explain them in a moment. First let's break apart the nucleus that makes logical sense simply from our history with COVID-19. The dates of when it started are a bit controversial so pick one:

December 31, 2019 or November 17, 2019

Either way it was declared a global pandemic by January 30, 2020.

As of when I'm writing this and the last report I could find states 217,813 deaths. 3,205,726 confirmed cases globally and this number seems to be fluctuating. Remember that population chart I had you draw? Take another look at it, we knew when a celebrity got sick didn't we? So is this number reflective of the elite? Or the mass majority out of that bottom chunk? The "stay-at-home order (aka a nice way of saying, "martial law") was issued 3-23-2020, beginning in *California*. Yes, heavily populated, but that is where the majority of the *elite* live yes? Hmm. Then let's look at the dates: 3-23-2020, 23=5; there it is. The rest of the country followed suit because sure we'll listen to Tom Hanks. But why? If they can keep enough of us inside, literally scared to leave, afraid to come near anyone even, what would be possible large scale? Just about anything! Mainly all stores are closed, sending in even more monitors, video cameras, spray everything down with…..? Calling it *decontamination*. Now that everyone's inside we can move large equipment around without anyone asking questions. Send up helicopters all day (check your local flight patterns, it's real), tell us the routes that are the less congested and at which times. Pay off all doctors anyone listens to then to falsely diagnose ailments as COVID-19 to keep that number on the rise. China was the first case; guess whose back to work and business as usual as if it was nothing? China. Odd right? Or is it with all the evidence, but everyone's asleep it seems. Now after 65 years of just reports out of Area 51, not to mention the years and places that belong to all of those "mentally ill" patients they let us have another distraction? Are they going to pay for every family's pain and suffering along with defamation of character/slander that has reported the exact same thing over the years? There is no justice; there is only what they want you to know, at that time. Because it seems now is the time we need to know what we knew all along, UFOs are there, I will say, just my personal minor interactions with this realm; nothing is or feels positive. For me it's always been hostile, insidious and incredibly beyond our intelligence of every manner. Now, I'll even take one for the team and go as far as to say perhaps this was a personal issue, or even just one species, but my conclusion and bias opinion. I'd like to think that all living avatar beings of any kind whether on this planet or not, all work for one energy source. That one sector has been just beyond my grasp of understanding and trust needless to say. Just from the one encounter I had, told me all I needed for a lifetime of never crossing paths again unless instructed to. Therefore I trust in profiling the whole sector the same. My path, their path, I don't fuck with you, you don't fuck with me is how I let that co-exist. Perhaps the government has made the same conclusion. We would be beat to shit, literally and almost instantaneously. However during this time of distancing and mask wearing, I'm left with an almost surge of hope for us as a species. We base most of a person's intentions on facial expression as well as body gestures, and have been cut off from this right now, it's covered in fact. I'm enjoying this because it cuts out the middle man of distraction and true intention is behind someone's eyes and feeling them across the room; which is something I can do very well, cutting out any bull-shit. I hope everyone is using this *setback* as a very valuable tool to move you/us forward in many ways. Feel your way through, it's our biggest asset; don't get bogged down with physicality when being touched comes in so many forms.

The men in black, to the three people who haven't seen the movie was a 1997 staring Tommy Lee Jones and Will Smith, Production Company was none other than Columbia Pictures and Amblin Entertainment. Amblin Entertainment if you just see their logo will remember it to be from you guessed it, ET. When Columbia Pictures first was becoming a name for themselves Harry Cohn (January 10, 1924), produced Walt Disney's film series from 1929-1932. As we all know W. Disney was a known anti-Semite and purchased the land for Disneyland with the help from the CIA. Got your tickets yet? Men in Black was/is a sci-fi action movie version of a true story, used to desensitize.

As reported the men in black are actual "men" dressed literally as the movie depicts; expressionless, cold in nature, rarely with any hair of any kind (brow, lashes, head etc.). these men appear at times of extreme phenomena, only talk to people whom have seen UFOs or people doing research or otherwise. As against propaganda and media I am, some things slip through and I wonder who they're meant for. Some motion pictures, music I think to myself, "fuck that's a sworn secret! How are they just laying it out there like that?" Then I see everyone around me not picking it up as I just did. Taking it just as pure *entertainment* value and going about their day. Some of it is a true story, whether it's labeled that way or not. Factual procedures missed with actors and performers under lights, cameras and cirque du soleil! Its madness! Truths and secrets sworn by real life practioners of both light and dark. Are they hidden then, is it a mocking of, or am I the only one who can decipher the code?

I will give you a great example of this, and it wasn't just me I don't think who saw it so see if you can see it as well. One the cover of the Beetles Sgt. Pepper's Lonely Hearts Club band, there's a lot to look at yes? A collective of very dark symbology in my opinion when you break it down, so let's:

Aleister Crowley past Poe that stuck out for me, not because he deserves any credit. He came before Anton Levey took over that sector in California.

Crowley born 10-12-1875 was a known occultist, did ceremonial magic, poet, painter, and novelist. He founded the religion of Thelema and appointed himself as the prophet (don't they all) guiding humanity into AEON of Horus.

In 1966 LaVey founded Satanism as an all-out religion and western esotericism (and probably the Denver Airport at this point). He was influenced mostly by two people, Friedrich Nietzsche and Ayn Rand. Crowley lived in Warwickshire and Levay grew up in Illinois before relocating to *California*, so there isn't much if any evidence these two had any "cross-paths."

Edger Allen Poe is on the album, and do I really need to go into him? Marilyn Monroe is just as obvious yet her birthday stands out: 6-1-1926. Her murder (8-4-1962) due to jealousy mixed with her knowing too much with a sprinkle of nervousness "someone" may get her pregnant that was important because she was basically used as human trafficking. Her birthdate adds down to a seven, figures; everyone wanted what she had, and judging by her birthday she wanted just to be her. Wanted nothing from anyone else. The day she died, fuck, burden and suffering, adding down four again creating wholeness out of suffering and burden, or that was the goal.

The remainder on the album:

"Huxley, Marlon Brando, Oscar Wilde, Hitler and Jesus (although never made it to the final print), Yukteswar Giri, Mae West, Lenny Bruce, Karl Heinz, Stockhausen, W.C. Fields, Carl Jung, Fred staire, Richard Merkin, Alberto Vargas, Leo Gorcey, Huntz Hall,

Simon Rodia, Bob Dylan, Aubrey Beardsley, Sir Robert Peel, Aldous Huxley, Dylan Thomas, Terry Southern, Dion DiMucci, Tony Curtis, Wallace Berman, Tommy Handley, William S. Burroughs, Mahavatar Babji, Stan Laurel, Richard Lindner, Oliver Hardy, Karl Marx, H.G. Wells, Paramahansa Yogananda, James Joyce, a hair dressers wax dummy, Stuart Sutcliff, another dummy, max Miller, "petty girl", Tom Mix, Tyrone Power, Larry Bell, David Livingstone, Johnny Weissmuller, Steven Crane, Issy Bonn, George Bernard Shaw, H.C. Westermann, Albert Stubbins, Lahiri Mahasaya, Lewis Carroll, T.E. Lawrence, Sonny Liston, "petty girl", George Harrison, john Lennon wax model, Shirley Temple, wax model Ringo Starr, wax model Paul McCartney, Albert Einstein, John Lennon holding a horn, Ringo Starr holding a trumpet, Paul McCartney holding a cor anglasis, George Harrison holding a piccolo, Bette Davis, Bobby Green, Marlene Dietrich, Mahatma Gandhi, wax model of Diana Dors, and a second Shirley Temple." (as if a single obsession with pedophilia wasn't enough).

Also on the cover is the following:

"A grandma figure, a doll replica of Shirley Temple with a Rolling Stones tee shirt on, a Mexican Tree of Life, Sony T.V., a figure of a girl, drumhead, hookah, snake, fukusuke, figure of Snow White (a nod to W. Disney perhaps?), a garden gnome, a baritone horn."

We all realize pedophilia is rapid within the elite, but do we ever dig as to why? Why children are targeted so hard as the bread and butter of commodity among these people. A representation of Shirley Temple here many times, and countless reports not only on the news but in your local neighborhoods and law enforcement agencies of CYFD and Crimes against Children. So why? A child's brain isn't fully developed in many ways as we all know in comparison to adults. A child looks to an adult for guidance, safety, reassurance and teaching. A skilled predator knows this and/or just realizes the loyalty and sees more opportunity. Before the turn of the century, children were viewed as second tier laborers and treated as if they were adults. Ancient Greek texts and hieroglyphics even depict younger and older together. It wasn't until probably child labor laws and not too long ago people as a whole started viewing children as individuals and precious growing minds and bodies. Yet for some reason, there are a vast number of people who still exploit their position as being an adult; what's worse, for currency or the occult.

I challenge you to break apart each of those individual's history, then cross reference them to how they would connect to one another, or what strengths they could gain. Note Prince changed his name to a symbol with a horn represented as well as always had the color purple somewhere. Guess what the universal color for the military is? What exploitation happened with some of those people, research what those items are used for in what ceremonies. Then look at that album cover again and ask yourself as I have, "Are you questioning my intelligence or pushing the envelope?" keep in mind how many points there are to that flower at the bottom left, as well as the number totaling fifty eight images depicted equaling or rather adding down to thirteen…which is four.

I've seen quite a lot, experienced too much at a young age, not to say my story isn't anywhere near in comparison to stories I've read or been exposed to. It's quite mild if you make a pie chart out if it then compared it against the world population of the truly horrific. Yet not much shocks or frightens me like what I'm about to explain. Yes, the sheer capabilities of some dimensions do, but I accept them, its beings that can travel within them that get me unnerved, and this is along those same lines.

In 1997, I saw a truly terrifying movie, it gave me the worst of the worst nightmares; I cried at night all of it. I've only seen it once; I don't plan to see it ever again. Now I've seen it all I think: Rosemary's Baby, Exorcist, Poltergeist, Cape Fear, The Birds, Deliverance, The Shinning, Psyco, The Omen etc. all before I was eight. Watching a thriller/sci-fi at the age of seventeen, let's just say I wasn't expecting much. The movie was Event Horizon staring Laurence Fishburne. It took two of my fears and stuck them in a blender and made them an actual possibility. Being in astronomy and learning about black holes almost brought me to tears in school. That combined with Dante's Inferno was basically splashed on the screen for over an hour and a half. It wasn't until last year I had an awake- nightmare when I read about Bootes Void, then it all came crashing back to me.

Black holes are one thing in astronomy and science, Robert Christner discovered something else entirely in 1981 upon accident. Approximately seven hundred million light years from Earth a three hundred and fifty million light years in diameter *void*. Not a black hole, a void that takes up approximately .27% in diameter of our observable universe (that we've known about for forty years). For an area in this location (located next to the Hercules, Draco Hercules, and Corona Super Clusters in the Bootes Constellation) of this size *should* contain at least tens of thousands of galaxies; but does not. Only sixty have been discovered after forty years of research and the patterns they possess aren't like anything we've come across, they are tube-like or sphere shaped.

Scientist love to say the following with a new discovery, "This suggests the universe is much older than originally thought." Yea, no shit, or our surroundings simply have been here millennia and we are a very young species.

Dark matter is nonluminous material in space that takes any form and/or high-energy moving particles created after the Big Bang theory. Is it possible Bootes Void is no more than this? Doubtful due to its collective of galaxies within it. Next it's been suggested it maybe the other side of a black hole we are seeing, and do I next ask, "What the fuck is on the other side?" I remembered black holes in three categories or sub-catagories: primordial, dark matter, and supermassive. To enter one would be death; the stretch of the worm-hole would no doubt shred every cell to nothingness. In my mind to think Bootes Void is the other side of one, is hard to grasp. The other disturbing fact about this, it's growing or if you want to look at it in another light, expanding outward. At present, although appearing to have a *boot* shape to most as does Ursa Major and Ursa Minor, I'm seeing five points as a star has; and I cannot un-see it.

Other things that this finding suggests are of separate civilizations, obvious. However, they've already been categorized and labeled in fact. A galactic civilization (type 3) or universal Civilization (type 4) where the A.I. have exceeded their host; which this void surely points to because no findings of much movement, sound, and the sheer evidence of shape.

AVATAR NATURE

Free will.

Plato and Aristotle started anarchy with that shit, an argument I'll take any day. Speaking of arguing, there is no talking anymore in my life. Just a series of arguments, I attempting to have a conversation and I noticing blasts of points getting across without no real ground being gained. Perhaps the people I'm around, unsure. But someone's always offended by SOMETHING. I researched the origin of free will back to the Bible and couldn't find a source. The prophet to whom gave it life, nothing. So it is assumed, never said as a rule. And Plato and Aristotle were the actual people to whom it was implied from. Which brought up a thought, how are priests, preachers, etc. saying it was God given? Am I not reading something? What prophet said these words? Did I miss it? I in my life do not have free will and that point gives me a twitching eye, sweat, vertigo and high blood pressure to explain to anyone. Why do I have to always explain myself to everyone? Then work on, usually in therapy, changing fundamentally everything about myself to fit in with society? Because I'm very outside all boxes and offend? Boxes are confined and go get a band aid! The rule has always been, you can't change the world, and you can only change yourself in the world. I understand this, but I HAVE to play both sides of that rule? Seems a bit fucked if you ask me. If we as a whole are moving to acceptance on a greater good, go all the way bitch. Accept that whole spectrum of human, not just the shades that go with your Prada. Let a bitch go to work with her head down with whatever expression gets her through that fucking day! Not having to speak to anyone, pick a lane! Who's Elaine? I am so damn confused and paranoid I don't know what's smarter to pack for lunch; smoothie for my hypothyroidism or a knife for the attacks! Do I gain 50lbs so no one touches me anymore or stay healthy and have to deal with yet another stressor? Yes, I've done this to remove me from the dating world. It works ladies, if you need a break, I don't support unhealthy eating habits-just saying. The black and white, no grey area I hear is part of my borderline personality disorder. I am told there is no grey area for us. Making it hard for relationships, compromise, jobs, you name it. But the questions I always have to this and will always have, "when has anything in history gotten done right in a grey area?" Well 50 Shades got some things right, not a lot, but the male casting, but even then there was a black and white contract! The law is black and white, not so much anymore. But when it goes astray it's usually grey right? Open your eyes to that concept for a minute. When a literal law, rule, boundary is not clearly understood as either black or white (let me change that term for you so it doesn't turn into a racial point because it's not) up or down, right or left (non-political) on or off. Whichever opposite you want to go with here, yes or no even. Fill in your own this isn't me being your therapist just making a point. Ok, so whenever it's not understood as such, and it blends into confusion of the two, everything in society, family, work, your emotions go wildly fucked! Yes or no? So I ask always, is it really me having a condition, or just a firm grasp on decisions? No questions, I fucking just pick one. Stick to it without too much emotion, otherwise shit gets messy. Examples of how we are led astray: love, family, work, the fucking police! You start out everything, with some sort of rule book. Life, work, family usually, relationships-sometimes, depending how this person is I guess.

I have the worst 1st dates. I'm a very sink or swim person, there's another comparison you can use. Get to the date, "I'll pay for myself, what I'm about to say you may or may not want to pay for. If you're holding and ace, I'll see it in approximately 20 min so trying to hold it in will only make it more apparent. The little family I talk to is what the world views as either crazy or low-lives; you will have little contact with them. I have two children, and unless I forgot and you were there, you are not their father. Respect and understand that on every level. Should I go or do you want to order?" Let's just say I'm alone, no one handles that well. Yes, it's funny, to me also. We have feminized men to the point where I, a woman, intimidate a man? What the fuck? Men were made to hunt! And now words are making them run away? Somethings very wrong. I'm taking a break after writing that so the aneurism heals.

Men used to be the strength. Women used to be the comfort. Now, in my eyes, they're blue, so this maybe a bit lighter than someone looking at it with brown eyes but men are tools (pun not intended) and women are providers?! Now I've got to rewire again? In technological aspects of earning I'll give you a small percentage for women. Yet, the capacity of women's emotions doesn't allow for providing entirely. They get caught up in grey areas, too sensitive. Can we be very valuable? Absolutely! We are masters at strategy! Strategy, manipulation, empathy, HSPs, INJFs. We are the natural form of lie detectors! But do men see and use this tool? Well that's where we all got pissed. That maybe the core of this women's rights crap. Which I'm behind to a certain degree, and with the correct backing. The one that is sociologically correct. The one that capitalizes on our born wizardry so to speak. Men forgot somewhere that they had the best tool to win battles over land, kings became greedy. Sev deadly sins started looking real good. Women then were burned by their talents, and thus started the great battle of sexes! Now shit is all blended and GREY! You've got men with women's powers, women with men's, you get to work on Thanksgiving and you don't know what to do. Should I cross my legs? I don't know! Guess I'm para-noid. If I eat the yams I'll be too woman later, can't do that. Why do you think mainly women were called witches? Just a thought, but maybe because we just knew, huh. Now, with that knowledge and men's power of physique and calmness to just simply carry out tasks.

Everyone gets a written "thing" when they begin something. You start a new job: here are the rules, polices, the procedures, even the outline of your job duties! School: syllabus, assignments, seating charts, bells (in case you don't own a watch), class schedule, maps to get there. I get so bat-shit crazy when someone shows up confused! LOOK IT UP! You were given the tools! I'll ask, until I'm blue tits, what is the fucking issue here? Do your job! You signed up for it, do it! Or the door is that way. What's with all the lip?! The confusion? The questions asking all the time?

Some of you ask, "what if I identify as Indigo?" THERE IS A PLACE FOR THE BLUE COLOR! I am not saying grey isn't great. No shade of anything in life is. But I will drive home my point here why it's a problem, and this has NOTHING to do with race. These are examples of personality issues I have and why. I'm using a fucking box of colored pencils as an analogy, so deal with it. So if you identify as 'indigo' what the fuck are you doing in the 'black n white' line asking confused questions? For starters, you're not fucking purple, your blue. So get that straight before you make yet another mistake by going over to the purple line and fucking up those peoples day. Quit asking me questions! I'm working on my policies, procedures they handed me day 1. As black and white d to the letter as I can. If you're confused, or lost, don't ask me;

I'm busy. If a complaint is what it is, get a therapist, sometimes HR is confused with being this person. They're not, get it straight. Above that, your boss is NOT by any means: your therapist, your chaperon, your FRIEND, an hour by hour checks in on tasks (or they shouldn't be). Your boss writes the checks. And if good at their position, doesn't need an hourly check in from their employees. Will know this automatically based upon hire and upkeep of what is produced. The only time you actually should talk to your boss is on major shifts, and turn in assignments. Do the job, don't half ass it. If you grow as a person, realize your more of another color, I get it. Move out of the line, do it on your own. Quit dragging the rest of us in our productive lines down with your issues. Some of us like our line. During sign up day, we were all excited to see what each offered. Agreed to terms, let us be please. Each line believes in that list, we don't care, or don't want to hear what you think of the list. You got problems, this isn't your line, but I'm not your therapist; don't treat me as such. I'm also not HR, and don't tattle to the boss I'm not willing to listen to all your bullshit. Not only have 'you' put everyone in an awkward position, but now somehow it's my fault. Still confused to this day on how that happens.

You can improve your list or charts in life, you cannot change them. Find new ones, can't usually change the idea or goals on the original. If so, they become a different color anyway; the old ones someone is always willing to keep up with. If your soul/spirit vibrates at another frequency, you'll just end up losing time trying to change it. Co-existing can only happen when you don't try to change anyone's fundamental chart or ethical list, but can admire and ultimately learn from it. Take notes for your list; let them copy off your quizzes for a unit test. Where the men and women dynamic is very handy. Children are very informative in a unit because of their simplicity. Staying current, and pure of heart in decision making. We forget to include them for these very valuable contributing tools. I wa silenced from birth until…not sure if that's ended. But, growing up in my grandparents' home, there was zero talk from those under a certain age, it was respect. If you were me, knew your place in the world very early and ready to get this shit done, it was hard in that house. The first decade was rough to say the least, the second was turbulent. I sat, with a piece of invisible piece of duct tape over my mouth for years. Had to only observe, listen. All that was said and done to me and around me happen. Good and fucking horrific in that, in everything. We need balance, not grey. I'm methodical as fuck because of that, systematic, compartmental. I had to be out of survival. If I wanted to learn ANYTHING, I'd mimic. If I missed seeing a step, I was fucked. So there I was getting yelled at for being stupid for not knowing how to do something while taking it apart and putting it back together. Me in silence.

In a democracy it's proper that a jury decides whether a crime has been punishable in a common law state aside from a civil law based on motivation and evidence. Not all crimes get a jury, some major offenses by the prosecution are not granted this luxury. It's not a luxury at all, is correct to invite the non-elite population to hear testimony that are not on any back door pay roll. "In the United States, jury trials are used in *serious crimes*," not to be confused with a "bench trial" where the judge or panel will then make the decision of verdict. Snowden knows this very well, and it's a crime within itself. The right to trial by jury in a criminal case is found in Article III Sec. II of Federal Constitution and the 6th Amendment. If you commit Espionage, not only is your 6th Amendment revoked but so is Article III. Even under the Whistleblowers Act of 1989, your **"Constitutional Rights are revoked to trial by jury."** For the simple fact of *its classified*, is all I can find. The jury-trial only applies when a serious offense (a sentence of more than six months in prison and penalties exceed penalties). What if the *classified* information vent the other way? It wasn't a threat to National Security; it was a threat on the American People by the government? Espionage is the only option under the Whistleblower's Act and what happens? Exactly, he still lives in Russia folks, and we do nothing. The part that blows my mind is none of you did anything with the information that was given and sacrificed for. Google is still our friend, Apple, people putting Alexa and Siri in charge as if this didn't happen. You have the information that was speculated on even before the proof was given, yet still funding the source? I'm confused why all the questions and confusion when shit goes south.

Cancer for example is genetically in all humans, yet I'm confused when anyone says, "I got cancer." You've always had cancer, do you mean, it came out of a dormant state? My follow up question then is, "What are you feeding it? Your PH levels?" Cancer thrives in acid, not alkaline, so what are you eating then? What happened to your immunity to drop with an acidic level to a point where cancer then became active?

Human beings are not capable of processing meat in our systems, we just aren't, sorry I know. It's the leading cause of the majority of our issues in cardiovascular, leaky gut and the list goes on. Adding to that list, we can't process dairy, flour, or sugar well or at all. I know you're thinking, "What the fuck is left?" But quite the contrary, it's what we only need, not crap we created to get in the way. It's about surviving, fueling the avatar. Every vegetable and fruit known to man plus an array of micro/macro-nutrients to supplement. Support the immune system at all costs, and remain alkaline. Baking soda is the quickest way to send a rampant active cancer cell back to hell! It's a neutralizer, sprinkle in a shot glass a day if you need to get it into the system. During my stage four, I went as far as bagging a continuous flow enema and douche plus shots of baking soda with lemon. Whatever it took to flush my system, needless to say, six biopsies later no live cancer cells could be found to move on to *mustard gas chemotherapy.* I've been there, I was my own lab rat and I'm still here today because I refused to do anything unnatural to save my system. If you have nothing to lose, and chemotherapy is literally putting your organs in a microwave all the while removing all of your immune system, which would you pick? I know the answer; you're on your way to the Apple store now and getting McDonald's on the way home in your Tesla. Which as the devil's symbol right on the tail I might add. Just sayin…

LAWS OF ANGELS AND DEMONS

Now that I've brought you from how "a crazy person becomes crazy" then homeless in America, let's talk about the other worlds. The ones I know more intimately it seems because the third dimension just pisses me off when I'm in it and truthfully I'm bored; the others are pure magic! Before I get into this, remember I was terrible in school. I have no degree no claim to have all the answers to the universe, but these are my observations being blessed enough to be shown answers. Now I can't explain that fully, but it's always been there. Just like I've always just literally known stories of the Bible before ever truly reading them or going to Sunday school. I literally don't know how I know things, or if they are true scientifically in your world, but after I've said them, look it up; fat check me. If I'm wrong, then I at least gave you some great thought about other worlds people live in, if I'm right....hm. Because this is just me writing, telling you what's been inside my head for four decades? Shit no one wants to listen to or give a shit to understand, which is fine; but I think it's fascinating.

There are argumentally eleven dimensions we know of. The first three are of space: length, vert and height. The fourth is of time. As human beings we have control over the first three dimensions of space; and live in the fourth right? If you observe our rapid moving technology, can see how our ego would like to dominate this dimension. We want to have super natural powers, so having control over time and space simultaneously would give us this capability. Allowing us to travel freely forward and backwards in time continuum; past and future. Keep in mind the only way this is not possible is because we are looking at it by moving a human (those cells and a cellular level) throughout that time and space. This is why it doesn't move; the vegetative cells a human is made up of is only able to move forward in the path its set to. When, or if it's disrupted, its cells would disrupt. The zero dimension has no length, no vert and no height; a point for example or dot. The first dimension is length, a line for example. The second or 2D objects are flat and can only move on a plane. Left, right, forward and reverse but not up and down; no depth; 3D is depth and in any direction. Without 4th degree nothing would take place as we know it in our minds. It's our point of origin of all start and stops; time. People focus on this one more than any other and I can't understand why, it's the one that humans get stuck on. Let's now move on to where most people don't live, focus, or even pay any attention; and in my opinion you should. In the 5th, standing in any given spot that location would look very differently. You'd be able to see the past and the future, the details of the 3rd that surround you. At 6D particles can be present at many places at the same time, so now you can replicate yourself as well as move in time at any direction. This is also where you meet parallel universes. At 7D, is infinite universes, and living here you'd be able to move through them or send a clone of yourself. The difference between the sixth and seventh dimension is the big bang theory whereas the seventh has no such laws to be able to move freely. At 8D things get possibly weird for folks, because you lose physical form. You cannot simply touch anything and vice versa and this is present moving up the ladder. At 9D, able to move in any universe at any time and own laws of physics apply here. 10D, my personal belief here is the face of your maker, or the maker of all the realms. Because now having explained all of that, that is power. I argue the eleven personally because I don't ever see where it fits but I could be wrong; there may be a quantum mechanical realm I'm always missing. So, where do "if aliens exist (they do) fit in" all of my theories here? My guess is always somewhere between six and eight depending on their technology. There are probably up in the millions of species, so where they all fit in each realm I can't say. During lucid dreaming and astral projection it's extremely easy to be in 5D and 6D. To meet beings in higher realms, your being needs to move right? If you both skip dimensions it's very possible to meet up on an astral plane or a place in the future or past.

Creating an illusion of "no way out" and closing in. Further and further, until sniffing out the victim(s) and going in for the kill. Look at evil's enemy and compare: Faith, love, family all push outward and try to grow. NWO tries to what? Get rid of symptoms, take away, kill, push out, and box. Toss a pill at any problem that can potentially be a treat to a genocide yes? Scaring the prey for the last one hundred years. Now we can't even talk! It's not in the crack house; it's in the white house folks. Not the pentagon, the pentagram, gets it straight. It's a clear fucking map; wake the fuck up and stop washing their pill down with fluoride, and pick up a book. Talk to each other. Smoke them out, don't run away, and hold a mirror up to everyone who cannot handle the truth! Its truth no soul that's dirty wants to look at. Take a long look at yours, come to terms with who you are and start showing others who they are. Make them answer for it, instead of chasing you. Stop them, dead in their tracks. Hold up a mirror, and see who sticks around. Huge, beings we truly are, not scavengers. Do not run from a circling bird, for you are not dying, make noise when you walk, let them hear you coming. The majority will scurry, most are cowards. However, some are brave and a spirit battle is necessary. Have no fear; they can't even bare most times to say their own name mush less look in that mirror. Remember what team you're on.

Have you seen the movie Lucy? The concept is amazing, the idea of using 100% of brain capacity yes? What if we weren't using our brain at all? Take the cellular level hindrance completely out of our own way? Since it cannot move through time, it cannot move past 7D, why use it? Why has it as a tool past 5D? Lucid dreaming proves this; astral projection proves this, even DMT! So why are we stuck, held back in our bodies? Why do we need our brains to comprehend it? Accept they simply cannot, feel your way through. Energy is vast and expansive; humans are 3D. Quit trying to fully understand it in this realm. Think of all of them moving together simultaneously, feel all of them, hear all of them, try to see everything.

Then someone speaks to you; are they past, present or future them? Are they aware they can move? Do they move at will? Are they human or something else entirely? Alien in human form, or demon? Angels can do this too. Are they simply a person brand new to Earth first round doing their first round of karma?

INFJs second nature is feeling, so putting this together with the first dominant pattern of intuition, human nature specific is extremely easy to forecast. This is all done subconsciously so it acts as almost a psychic ability. This personality wants things to be perfect and live in fear of failure at all times. They procrastinate due to this because if they cannot surpass the norm of greatness why do it right? At the same time criticism is rough on them because the things they do set out to do they did with all their abilities. These people value beauty and quality over quantity. Sophistication usually surrounds them in all they do or there is an aspect of it in it; but tend to be minimalists. Deepest darkest secrets will be shared with these individuals even when you didn't mean to do to their charm and warm nature, but they're incredibly trustworthy. Since they can meet people and understand their emotional state in seconds, they can communicate and empathize; even help them move in another direction. Getting to know an INFJ isn't as easy as you may think however, the surface 's clear, but while they're helping you with your problems let's say;

they're digging behind why your brain is reacting in such a way. Peeling away all the layers of you and decoding them like a science project. Labeling and storing in memory like a computer. Simply because it fascinates them, all the while setting up boobie traps along the way behind them incase they're dealing with another INFJ of a higher dimensional being trying to crack codes!

It's hard for them to know if it's their emotions or others. Feeling the entire room, it becomes hard who's belongs to whom. Introverts by nature and sensitive to conflict. Yet all of the opposites of these they can either fake or do well, the preference is alone and calm. Can you see the similarities of an INFJ and a BPD? I could even go one further for you, should I? I'm going to now give you some characteristic and paint yet another picture to make a point.

This person tends to be loyal to a fault, sophisticated, independent, unique, artistic, and on point judgement. They strive for independence and refuse anyone or anything that holds them back. Freedom to pursue what they want when they want is number one. Love to travel and great innovators. These people do tend to isolate themselves due to independence; their spontaneity and randomness comes just from being bored. Emotionally intelligent equips them to connect them with diverse people around them; enabling them to dig deep quickly and see the bigger picture and help those around them. They cannot take criticism; over confident in their abilities makes them sloppy. Incredibly compassionate people, sometimes volatile. Brutally honest even when you don't want to hear how badly it is. Tactless and arrogant, both are words this person hears too frequently, but it is their no-bullshit-get-to-the-point-move-on nature that drives them more rather than your opinion of them. They did fine without you, they will move on without you just fine. But not without 100 questions why first. Curiosity is this person's greatest downfall. Dissection is the key, to learning its every mov

and motivation as to how to deal with it in the future fuels this individual. I could go on, but you get a glimpse yes? Now, I ask, this
person goes into a therapist office and gets diagnosed with probably
something needing medication based on those characteristics. You
want to know what it is? Traits of the astrological sign of Sagittarius!

Do individuals have mental illnesses or simply categorized simply for
even a birthdate? Interesting right? Is it a pro or a con, really? Are we
medicating and therapizing "issues" just to make a buck? When truly
it's an astrological birth chart, or personality trait, or DNA? Every
single one of us is given a code and chart when coming here; complete
with numerology and coding. That chart is full of pros and cons, both
light and dark trust me. Just as the contracts we agreed to before coming here, each experience molds our original coding into something we
need to become. Now I ask, if you stop this process, cosmically, think
your ill in some way rather than allowing it to flow who then are you
letting you become? A conduit! Refusing who you are, medicating it,
labeling it, is all suppression. Just like pushing away negative feelings
or circumstances. Stick with me here, I'm not saying allowing bad
things to go ahead and happen to you, or walk out in traffic. But we all
know someone who says, "I don't like bad vibes," or "I can't be around
bad energy." That asshole am I right? I ask, why? How much of your
good energy are you spending running from it? THE WORLD IS
FILLED WITH BAD ENERGY! The day in fact, there is no escape.
So don't run, use it. I appreciate each negative just as I do the positive,
because it was given as a gift. Those are the moments to ask, "Why
did I (God) send this to me?" "What am I to learn?" Instead of being
reactive to the people doing it (unless of course they're attacking) I'm
deeply thinking of why it was sent to me. If I'm highly emotional, I
know there's a lot of baggage tied to that encounter I'm going to keep
experiencing unless I process it properly. I thank everyone involved
for bringing it to my attention and do my very best to work out the
ghest emotions first. This is how you handle stress and negativity,

because not all stress is bad; there's eustress and hormesis. Exposure to low dose stimuli over long or short periods of time to see how you respond is what life does for you. In a therapy session it's called PTSD, so I'm confused as shit! Eustress is the good responses; anytime you're anxious for something good to take place. It's still cortisol, dopamine, adrenaline; terrible shit pumping through your body but for good reasons. I hope we all know what we need to do with that at this point yes? We know any inflects of dopamine good or bad the avatar needs to release it in a form of burn off yes? Put your hamster on a wheel, jerk off, go fuck, something. Shit, do both of these at the same time and save you some karma time!

I know I just mentioned zero medication for mental illness and that may have you shaken or freighted even. A looney reads this, flushes his bottle of thorizine, and hops on the bus to work with you tomorrow giving you the stiff one eye trying to "process negative feelings solo." I can see both sides, I can. But can you? Have you put yourself in our world yet? Feeling completely shunned by everyone you meet? Everyone is literally a stranger, an unknown in the millions of dimensional realms a stranger. To do harm, not to? Some wanting to force pills down your throat, sounds like a scary government experimental movie right? This is where many of us live, right now. On the out skirts, but we're here. Watching, observing, knowing yet do we tell ya the truth? Do you listen when we speak? We're just crazy right?

Welcome to my world.

There are four degrees of an actual full blown possession; it takes time. You see this number a lot due to its numberology of its meaning and we will get into that. The first wave comes with infestation of a demon or darker force of any kind. I personally do not give any energy the label of a demon specifically until it gives me their name, for I know not which realm they are from. At this stage you will get footsteps, hearing voices, apparitions, objects being moved unexplained, smells, and pets noticing odd things. Objects being tossed around and nothing ever moving to the next level is simply a poltergeist. An entity only capable of moving objects from our realm of vision and living in its own; think fifth dimension. The next wave is obsession, and just like the word implies, it fixates on a person. The individual has then a harder time with this avatar reality. Changes in functionality, sleep, stuck in thought, and suicidal ideations. This stage is tricky yet has some highlights that make it very clear. An n person who is becoming enlightened has almost the exact same tendencies! What's different? Expansion vs. regression, abundance vs. extinction. At times these can be muddy to confuse those around them. Finally possession is last however not fatal. A great deal of judgement and coherent abilities have been removed yes, but the goal up to this point having gone through the stages having taken weeks or months (years even) is to have broken the individual down so much that you give up. By giving up, this can be anything ranging from suicide to murder, even sacrificing another being. This phase also includes the person knowing other languages, body metamorphosis, and adversities to objects and extensive knowledge of other's life and events not known previous. Now, notice I said objects, not specific to "the crucifix" here. Not all entities are created equal, and again just because one is of lower force or there to do unjust to the person, doesn't make it a "demon." Until it labels itself, I then do not. It's just energy until something infuses it with a scent; level grounds until then. Notice objects it responds to giving clues to what you're dealing with. Every angel and demon has been given a name upon creation, just like to our parents giving them the push on what our names were at conception. All beings have a name; however, darker forces love giving themselves human names vs. their given ones to mask who they truly are. Just like they like to call themselves demons when they're not even of that rank. So don't give anything energy it doesn't deserve just because it feels it's entitled. I assure you, it's not even worth handing over that much respect if games are what it's doing. If you're dealing with a being that's skirting, not giving you its identity, then I suggest not entertaining it with infusions and delusions of grandeur. Move on to doing your work and why you're there, speed it up; no time for shenanigans. Some knowledge into the goat and its meaning, because not only is it around, but it will be prevalent. In the thirtieth and fourteenth centuries, the Knights Templar adopted a half-human half-goat deity that was named Baphomet. However prior to that it was first mentioned in eleventh century in a letter by a crusader named Anselm of Ribemont. Speed all that up to present time, 1966 along comes Anton Levay, he takes the deity and calls it the "Sigil of Baphomet" and fuck here we go satinists! Now, aside from who adopts what and turns it into whatever, before something gets infused it's generally a basic symbol on its own. The star for example, representing the elements of earth, air, fire, water and spirit yes? Also the male and female, but more so in the Jewish Star of David. You turn it upside down, infuse it, slap it on the head of a deity goat and pray to it, sacrifice ceremonies; now the symbol has been invoked. Once turned upside down, a huge group of people turned a once very meaningful symbol into something dark. Even though everything has an opposite automatically, just as every Angel has their counter, now Baphomet stands for something else; and I'll break it down for you. one point at the top to the white moon, the other down to the black moon, one arm is female the other male, flame of intelligence between the horns, the head is the horror of the sinner, a rod for a penis meaning eternal life, body in scales, a semi-circle above in the air, usually breasts showing androgynous. If you break it down, its dualities show all life or in all things and this being pointing out the line or of confusing what black and white. Again here we are in grey areas! Their symbol is black and white, yet they move in grey; interesting don't you think? I pose one thought, who do we all work for? Exactly...

NAVIGATION

I'm often accused of being paranoid, mocked under the heading in fine print of the title: Borderline Personality Disorder aka mental illness as a symptom. As already discussed, I feel its bullshit in a lot of ways; but let's hoan in on paranoia. When you take a spirit or energy, whichever you believe and place it in an avatar of a human it goes to sleep so to speak. So the following will be very esoteric, but try to follow along with an open mind.

As children we are told this is who we are; this body, this mind. To use and learn own senses right? Anything to better use and focus on those senses, therefore making us more into our body. Further away from the truth of an immortal energy living in an avatar can do. More importantly, this avatar is at a low vibration! Something our higher self isn't used to vibrating at. Time and space are new, negative thought, severed connections to any and all things are hindered, yet every being is multidimensional whether they are aware or not. Earth was chosen because of its third dimension reality, ecosystem for the avatar, and vibrational pulls. However because it's in the third dimension, this is why the "dementia of the avatar to spirit" happens. Time and space exists here. There is a time laps, you feel you know it but can't remember the picture. Trust the feeling, trust every déjà vu. Always your avatar glitching and your spirit

awakening. Remember you chose to forget, chose this paradox for
a reason. All charts made prior to avatar birth were unique. Earth
is the contract of Karma, and you chose it. Every horrid thing you
have ever been through, you chose it. More importantly, and here's
the kicker, you already planned doing it with that other spirit/person
prior to getting here. Did I say you and your rapist planned it out
with details prior to your births? No, I did not, so calm down. I am
saying, whatever karma you had prior to being attacked needed to
work out in a gruesome way that taught you finally in this realm
what needed to be taught. It took a horrid thing to get the point
across. I've been molested and raped, and in no way am I advocat-
ing it should be free-reign here. I'm saying it's bigger than the act of
victim. I've been to this realm many times, and had plenty done to
me; here and there. I own my part as best I can, where I signed on
for the karma. If I'm hard-headed too much the first time around to
get it, I'll be cycled through again to get it worse. The abuser had to
sign up for it too; I understand that; it's not my spirit they do damage
to. Kick around the avatar, that's fine; it's borrowed. If I don't absorb
everything I can from this, my spirit has to relieve it. End of chart.
Do we ever get a chance to shed the avatar and communicate with
our higher self or others? Of course! When you literally put your
avatar to sleep, astral projection, DMT, deep meditation, deprivation
tanks, and lots of combinations of the above. You, we, were all born
into the avatar with a map also. So no one is lost and alone without
help, without direct guidance from God, you and other spirits.
You're simply not. Dates, times, places were all given to your human
form to help you. Just as other humans, it's again up to you not to
ignore them. Learn to allow tools to be given; learn to use the ones
you have to the fullest. Then you walk the line, that path you chose
here. Finally awake, understanding what it all means right? What
every encounter may possibly mean, who is trying to tell you what.
Who sent them; are they here for karma of yours or theirs? Because
that's out there. A lot of what we take on for sympathy or empathy

out of love isn't even our own karma! Chew on that co-dependent people in the world. And that's a huge grey area to sift through to find what belongs to you. Build a mate up, support their journey, but don't get lost in what's not yours is a BIG test. In every relationship. Most can't handle you, or I, have a cutoff point. Sorry, I have a reason for being here. It's bigger than you. Call me selfish if it helps you sleep at night, I never sleep, I'm working; I have purpose. Back to my main point of paranoia. Some, we'll all, call this manic paranoia. I see it as complex awareness in a world that's mostly asleep. Very finely attune with my full capabilities up to this point. Where are you? Is that a judgmental statement? Oh I've been accused of that too. It should be a motivational question; because we ALL are. Ask yourself, at any point, if a judgmental remark or statement has ever been made in history, why it offends instead of motivates you. This is a lower dimensional planet for a reason, remember; so think about that. If a negative force makes you react negatively you are not ascending to move past that karma. You will get it again, worse. Then again, bigger. Until you react. The subtle inflects of vibration at the beginning is where you pay attention. Miss those, and you can't move forwards with ease. Understand? This is just karma and same plane spirits with us though. We all are battling angels, demons, aliens and I'm sure plenty I'm not developed enough to fathom yet. They're all on their own paths as well; separate from why humans are here. It can be mixed, but definitely on another flight path. I can assure one thing, from personal experience, demonic entities do not want awareness. Nor any spirit to use full capacity for karma charts. They work tirelessly at keeping us here. Now after explaining all of that, am I paranoid in your opinion?

I can hear, personally, the conversations inside people's hearts. Not words, but I can hear the feelings behind them. It's hard to explain, put me in a room with many people and it becomes too overwhelming. "They" call this BPD, but you are the judge. It's a

damn good, if learned, survival skill everyone needs. If I was born
with this gift, it's also a curse. I can't enjoy large gatherings of any
kind. But wouldn't want to. I hear children louder and easier, and
have a bigger connection to them as well as the elderly; they sound
the same. In the middle age range, I hear every horrid thing either
people have done or want to do. Or the pain in what's been done to
them; a war of inner deviancy and malice that goes on in a crowd.
It's truly stomach turning, but because I'm aware, its scary thinking
of which frequency I'm listening to. Is this their avatar on a higher
dimension, are they aware of it? Are they in control of their avatar?
If not, then that could be anyone I'm hearing with those thoughts. If
I'm hearing, probably something in the crowd can hear me too right?
And it happens, I catch eyes hearing me listening in, a recognition of
vibration. It's almost a respect glare I get, sometimes a challenge. I do
not like those, simply because you don't know what you're dealing
with and from where. I'm confident in protection in my being, yet
the battlefield is unpredictable. It's not 100% carnage either; you
hear lust, even very innocent gestures of love. I'll be honest, it's rare;
but it's there. I'll tell you what I almost never hear, and it makes
me cry when I do; is the sound around someone's heart of God and
spirit. Don had that at all times, and it was truly beautiful to be in
his presence. It's hard to talk to people, form sentences with them.
the shouting of their story, or future wants, the person's sitting next
to them or across the room gets louder depending on how pent up
they are.

I do believe in medicine to enhance the avatar that this dimension
provides that isn't man made. Those were put here to guide us just
as our charts were given to us. Macronutrients and micronutrients
enhance this body in ways you'd never imagine if taken religiously.
Plants are our best survival and we thrive on everything they can do
for us. That said, with the power of our own spirit and connection
with others combined with acceptance vs. reacting to this world

and people. Always ask what is the end goal, in everything. What's the take away, what am I to get from XYZ? If there's a goal there's a way through. Then you can navigate the emotion a hell of a lot easier, the reactions are easier. You can go into auto pilot a bit with the plan, while you're doing it tell yourself thank you. Because you are doing a great job at remaining calm at accepting this isn't easy. But also thanking you for sending it to you too, or go bigger and thank GOD! Who you made the contract with anyway; you're just doing the work. People will hurt you, challenge you, and get you to second guess yourself like a mother fucker. But that's the point, who do you remain? Do you let it go in one ear and out the other without a flinch of reaction? If not, process that bitch immediately, because there should be zero reaction to who you are and why you're here. If your character is questioned, or an aspect of it and you react, sit on that. It's not them, it's you. Nothing anyone says or does should have any impact on why you're here; there should be zero upset or reaction on words for sure. Got through them, if a person makes an observation of you/about you it's simply that. Now, if it bothers you, not them. People can say and observe all the live long day. It's up to you to accept that. I observe, but that doesn't hold any merit to any issues with what I'm observing. It's always the listener that has the problem, don't be that person. Change the world; flip the narrative into something useful to your growth. Work on your issues damn it; they aren't everyone else's problems. Some are, plenty are; but don't add to it. It's very grey out there folks. Big families are the worst, I feel for you guys. My shit is now belongs to you, why? Because we're family? No fucking way! I'm here on this realm doing my dirty work; you deal with your shit. We share blood yes, but stick to your side.

THE END OR THE BEGINNING?

I've spent all of my life up to a point or place hiding who I am for other people. That meant hiding from people I love and people that could have loved me. Locked myself up in seclusion because I know what any relationship causes, work or otherwise.

I feel myself bitter at trans/gay rights now, not that I have one thing against them, but that if a society has made room over time for such a concept, why "mental issues" ben just as accepted? If it is what I have.

Yes, even on applications they have preferences on gender, yet if you have borderline personality, PTSD, bipolar disorder or mania does it give you a box? No! You have a disability, that's a violation in my book, this book if none other. I didn't ask for this, nor did anyone who is gay. Yet the platforms aren't disability vs. human being. A disable bipolar is forced to take medication for his. That's absurd. Do you have any idea how hard it is to find work if you have a mental illness? Next question, how hard it is to keep a job? It's a ticking time bomb every minute at work. Not to yell, throw things, curse, and say a wrong word in the new dictionary that just came out under free speech that now people somehow cannot say them anymore due to increasing sensibilities. But we need to be accepting? It's infuriating! Must conform right?

There's Trans pride and gay pride and I love to see that happening, but it doesn't come without a part of my brain without resentment. Not for those people, but with jealousy. That will never be us. Ask anyone who has an acute mental illness disability. Ask if they feel like a huge part of them always needs to be hidden, being edited before we can truly speak.

I'm not stating that the take away from this entire thing is by any means all disable mentally ill people are ticking time bombs waiting to pull any trigger in a crowd or last confrontation. Granted, the right recipe is; but as a mass group of people in my opinion (not a medical one) we are on a hair trigger, feeling pushed back in the "crazy box." Toss some pharmaceuticals down our throats; keep us quiet, functioning, workable citizens. When truly putting a foot on the tiger's neck. You know the story of the circus tiger yes? Chained, wiped and caged to do tricks for its master for show after show. Waiting for that one night, one weakness in the routine. Then attack! Why is it always a shock? You beat an animal down, strip him of all natural rights, force him to obey at command, and yet expect a different response? Why in God's name would you try to do this? To any animal first, yes I'm pro-animal rights, but then attempt to think you can have slaves? Move forward in time, create pills and still have this hierarchy! This is across the board, not just with mental issues, health, geographic, race, social, or economic. We call this country Land of the Free, but it should read Little Babushkas. It's what we represent, not on paper we wouldn't want to look like assholes. But right underneath the surface; its segregated and silenced and very taboo. Social classes, the non-educated, the judged, the elite, the poor; it's all there. Then the mothership, the drone that keeps this madness per capita, technology.

That sexy, shiny, high ticket price tag bitch keeping all the evil swirling. Bonus, making a profit off stupidity. Because the further man gets from not only ourselves as a base being, but as human, the closer to shackles we are in. You are not dependent on any machine, whether it is a corporate one, a pharmaceutical one, a family one, a technological one, a social one, economical, or government. Yes I said that shit. The machine you were born with, trust where it came from, feed that. Take a knee to that power source. Beg not to be struck down daily.

I'm asked a lot why I don't stand for the pledge, my simple answer is, "it's religious." When I'm not religious at all, yet simple minds in passing can comprehend this quickly. It's because I don't believe in pledging, vowing, or taking any sort of oaths that aren't for God. I sure as shit will not be doing it in a mass of people that is vitally intimate. I will take a knee though, and I don't care where I am if this is required of me. I'm never sorry if this offends anyone, I know my truth. I urge you to seek not only yours but the vast facts around you in your environment every day; most are not so veiled. Where has everyone's wires gotten crossed?

I start feeling like MI6, "who do you work for?" Self, the system? Under a light in interrogation, what the fuck is going on? You're judging ME?! But you're signing with the congregation? That supports genocide? I'm the problem? Oh I just need to take a pill, okay. Wipe out my crazy thoughts and theories....that you did? That's not confusing. This idea that free will is a choice or even a concept is absurd. Free will is chaos, going against our literal charted order of numbers and map to keep it in line. It's very clear how black and white and simple it is. When does it become complicated? When everyone wants to live in a grey area of anarchy. We don't decide the reality that is, it's already there; yet we can manipulate the avatar into ten dimensions. However this ability shouldn't be ours to toy with without a higher permission and/or pull from the other side. To force a butterfly's flap of its wings can only cause a tidal wave. It's true in science, its true in human nature, it's true in relationships. The only real push we do have control over is our own paths, and even that must first be waited in line for.

God at the beginning of time made order out of ciaos, it was then our misconception we had any right to then freely manipulate it. Just because it was written every Angel bowed to this creation called man, goes not give us the right to become narcissistic in character or lose respect for our soldiers. No creation at any level is better or worse than the other, everything is working under one boss; all realms, all levels. If it's not, it's simply lost on its map, lost in grey matter. An influx of over emotion, frustration, range, erratic behavior, a glitch in the matrix even, or otherwise is simply a form of oppression; a fork in the road on your map, where it should always come back to clear. It's ok to get lost, but don't wander; we are all on mission, too busy to become lost for long. See the clear signs at the fork in the road, for they are not a fork at all, yet simply an illusion of time continuum or insidious oppression.

I hope you can see my frustration, the absurd contradictions and outward bullshit of it all. Again I hope this will spark your own research on every topic, the paths they form, the manipulation of it all. Listen closely to phrasing, key words mean everything when forming clues to underlying real intentions.

Houdini's greatest trick was misdirection.

Houdini 3-24-1874 = 2 = dual nature.

Just sayin…

LETTERS TO THEM

Flying Monkeys –

You knew who you were, you loved telling me. It seemed, if not just apparent to me, you were very secure in who you were and what you stood for. Something many people struggle with, I sheered you on for it. I never had room to, and massively mocked for. Something we had in common and one of many. You wore who you were like a badge of honor! But what I admired most is how you did it, with a smile. The good, the bad, and the fucking scary at times, you came out with one mission; and did it with a smile. The inner monologue of that I watched in amusement of awe. Perhaps it was that, or your sheer size physically no one dare challenge. However I was envious of both. I still to this day see you and I as drama masks if you will in the world. It just so the coin got tossed, I was Melpomene to the outside and you had Thalia. Yet it seemed to reverse in private, or perhaps we just knew which mask the audience needed per event. Quite the trickster if yin yang we were, yes? Ironic how we both were labeled as "crazy" and "mentally ill" by many, yet we were the people others would seek for answers when lost. They'll never admit it, but it's the truth. This brings me to the cry out to my partner each day. I know you're frustrated with me, I know I'm doing several things wrong, I know I haven't been listening. I know a lot, but on that note, I'm navigating without my fucking compass! I'm in a human avatar, considering which you are to me, the work we were doing; how important it is, and what it means. The facts remain I'm pushing my avatar in this matrix further than ever before and had four symbolic attempts on my life, please understand how I am coping. Instead I get frustration from you, and I don't know why. What am I not completing correctly? And by writing this, I got my answer. I'm not ready to accept that, I won't write what you said here, that's just for me. But I do understand, logically. I can't do as you ask yet; I fear I'll never hear you again; never feel you in almost everything I do. I can't go back to doing this alone, this work. I get we're all alone, but we were a gift to one another. A borrowed gift at best, but I haven't processed all we were and meant yet. Ok, I have but I just haven't packed it up, labeled it and decided to move it out. Please be patient, or more patient with me. I have literally pockets of time dedicated to you before something else swings out of my favor as you know. Compassion please. I know what has to be done, and I'll complete the task, try to make a deal where my fear of not hearing or feeling you doesn't disappear. I don't know how to do this without you; I depended on you far too much now to be left completely naked in Times Square. I am literally crippled mentally simply because you kept me calibrated. What used to be fluid is now become a million times harder with results of silence. The science behind that I simply cannot figure out. The best parts of my life were the ones with you.

Rubber Ducky –

When I was a young girl I'd write down lyrics to songs, copy poems and stare at the words because the words were so powerful to me. Music especially I thought, "I wonder what it'd be like to have a feeling so powerful for another human to write words like this." I'd look at classmates and couldn't imagine it, it seemed almost false. People were very vapid in my opinion, no inner monologue or irony or where we were even going on their heads at all times. Just going through the motions of existence; I found this maddening, and still do in fact. I imagined being followed by a man from another time, another place far away I'd never been. Filled with culture, music and people who dressed differently; I talked to him about great poets. Whitman, Poe, Shakespeare and picked apart music lyrics of the Beetles and the Stones. Imagined him listening to music with me and walking home from school speaking to me in my head. Through the years I kept him in this box, it was sage and my experiences were not, he could read my mind and never took advantage of me or used me for gain of selfish reasons. As I got older the terms "the one" or "soul mates" where tossed around and I thought, "If my imaginary man from another time became real, I could see it." All my bullshit would lay down for him, in a calm whirlwind of thought vibration with a smile. Now I've had experiences where you meet people and you can't remember your name introducing yourself because of the vibrational intensity, but the ones that reroute your entire life meaning moving forward leaves you imprinted. Upon our first meeting, it almost felt wrong to shake his hand. I couldn't make eye contact, not because he was particularly attractive but because I respected him. He came from another place; he had history and spoke in pure poetry. His presence was a time warp where it either stopped completely or travelled quickly. We were both addicted to that feeling because each kept looking to plug it back in. Yet I noticed silence was okay too, it was just the energy that was simply like heroine. To have someone inside your mind, in all the dark corners of fear and insecurity to then come out the other side to tell you he enjoys it as much as you do; is erotic. All the while mentally brushing your hair and reading you poetry during the ride. During the time it was so innocently encapsulated without a touch. I saw what a small piece of the world he wanted to be in and vice versa.

Dream existences, music, pasts, religion, sex, trauma on both ends. But we couldn't look each other in the eye, one would always look away. Now moving forward, I cannot imagine anything less; perhaps I created this imaginary man to be in my life and manifested it for real even for a brief time, or simply to teach me a great lesson once again. A hard one. It's all in your head. Making him up, any real love or connection, anyone who would truly accept or love you for who you truly are and be able to touch you after knowing. Losing your way so badly to find a fellow traveler from another time only to then send you packing when you lose the map. Now I'm left with silence, abstinence and a feeling in the pit of my stomach he still feels me as well. If that's true, I hope he asks himself one question, "why?" Why was the energy there? Furthermore, why he continues to fight against it? But like I said, it must be just my imagination right? A figment of my imagination of someone I created as a kid that doesn't exist because how possibly could he? And as Stevie Nicks said, "You've left me now and it's seasoned my soul." But if I drilled a hole through the earth directly from where we are now to the opposite side of the planet, I may see you in the Indian Ocean between Madagascar and Australia.

Printed in the United States
By Bookmasters